FROM A
COLONIAL GARDEN

FROM A
COLONIAL GARDEN

IDEAS, DECORATIONS, RECIPES

By Susan Hight Rountree

Photography by Tom Green

Illustrations by Elizabeth Hundley Babb

Line drawings by Susan Hight Rountree

Colonial Williamsburg
The Colonial Williamsburg Foundation
Williamsburg, Virginia

Library of Congress Cataloging-in-Publication Data

Rountree, Susan Hight.
  From a colonial garden : ideas, decorations, recipes / by Susan Hight Rountree ; illustrations by Elizabeth Hundley Babb ; photography by Tom Green ; line drawings by Susan Hight Rountree.
     p. cm.
  ISBN 0-87935-212-4 (hardcover : alk. paper)
 1. Floral decorations—Virginia—Williamsburg. 2. Nature craft—Virginia—Williamsburg. 3. Cookery—Virginia—Williamsburg. I. Title.
SB449.R68 2003
745.92—dc22
                                              2003019671

Published in 2003 by
The Colonial Williamsburg Foundation,
P.O. Box 1776, Williamsburg, VA 23187-1776
www.colonialwilliamsburg.org

Designed by Helen M. Olds

Printed and bound in Singapore

Contents

"Some one always coming to perfection."—Thomas Jefferson

To the Reader

"No occupation is so delightful to me as the culture of the earth, and no culture comparable to that of the garden. Such a variety of subjects, *some one always coming to perfection* . . . though an old man, I am but a young gardener." So wrote Thomas Jefferson, whose passion for gardening lasted a lifetime.

Many colonial Virginians shared his passion. Two of the most impressive gardens were found in Williamsburg. Visitors and townspeople alike were no doubt enthralled with those established by the royal governor and by John Custis, a leading citizen and landowner who was reputed to have the finest garden in Virginia. Many of the other gardens in town were not as extensive and were planted by merchants and tradespeople who cultivated vegetable gardens with herbs and flowers scattered throughout. They often added small orchards if they had space.

The mixture of flowers, vegetables, and fruits in colonial Virginians' gardens is reported by Philip Vickers Fithian who tutored Robert Carter's children at Nomini Hall. On March 16, 1774, he noted in his diary: "After school, I had the honour of taking a walk with Mrs Carter through the Garden—It is beautiful, & I think uncommon to see at this Season peas all up two & three Inches—We gathered two or three Cowslips in full-Bloom; & as many violets—The English Honey Suckle is all out in green & tender Leaves—Mr Gregory is grafting some figs—Mrs Carter shewed me her Apricot-Grafts; Asparagus Beds &c."

Today, nearly 250 years after Jefferson came to Williamsburg to attend the College of William and Mary and saw the town's gardens for the first time, "some one" flower or herb or vegetable is still reaching for perfection. The number, variety, and charm of the gardens make the town a destination for ardent gardeners from around the world. Because of Tidewater Virginia's benign climate and fertile soil, the gardens yield a great assortment of vegetables, flowers, foliage, and fruits. Their beauty and bounty inspired the ideas, decorations, and recipes on the following pages. I hope you will try some decorations, experiment with new recipes, preserve flowers, herbs, and foliage to enjoy in the winter months, and create a topiary to keep fresh your memories of this green country town.

Above and opposite: Gardening tools and techniques are shown at The Colonial Garden and Nursery.

COLONIAL WILLIAMSBURG'S GARDENS

From the regal grounds of the Governor's Palace, with pleasure gardens fit for the King's representative in Virginia, to the simple kitchen garden at the James Geddy House that sustained not only Mr. Geddy, but also his wife, children, and servants, Williamsburg's gardens have always played a significant role in the life of the town. They are still important in portraying life in eighteenth-century Virginia.

At The Colonial Garden and Nursery, located on Duke of Gloucester Street across from Bruton Parish Church, costumed gardeners young and old will show you eighteenth-century-style tools and accessories, including handcrafted rakes, wheelbarrows, and enormous baskets made by Colonial Williamsburg's tradespeople. Watch them make serviceable yet decorative woven fences—a good idea for your borders—and put in rows of saplings on which to grow peas. You will see cold frames, glass bell jars, and straw

1

domes protecting tender seedlings as they emerge in the early spring. Later, you can apply these techniques at home. Children will be drawn into gardening activities by interpreters their own age during school breaks and in the summer. Junior interpreters will recruit help to plant, water, and weed crops including broccoli, which the young guests may even get to like.

You will learn old cooking secrets from the gardeners. For instance, do you know how to cook cardoon, or even what it is? Cardoon, which is related to the artichoke, was cut up and added to soup or steamed in water and vinegar, then quickly sautéed in olive oil. Artichokes, highly prized, were prepared much as they are today.

Salsa lovers will be surprised to discover that peppers were grown in eighteenth-century Williams-

Peppers are tended by a colonial gardener.

Artichokes were a great delicacy in eighteenth-century Williamsburg.

burg. Native plants and those introduced to Tidewater Virginia, such as the pepper plant, can be purchased in season to put in your garden or to use in recipes or decorations (see pages 14, 52–53, and 118).

The Colonial Garden is burgeoning with ideas. You will have a chance to become familiar with the many herbs, from their habits and appearance to their scents and flavors. You can later take home one or two unfamiliar ones to plant in your own garden. Acquire a bell jar to protect your young seedlings or make a hanging lantern (see page 205). Consider adding a pathway of crushed clam and oyster shells, like the ones you see throughout the Historic Area.

Much of what is known about crops that were planted in colonial Virginia and how and when to plant them comes from John Randolph's *A Treatise on Gardening.* Randolph was a prominent citizen of Williamsburg prior to the Revolution and an avid gentleman gardener. Many of the crops and methods in his book are demonstrated at The Colonial Garden. In his fascinating journal, Randolph not only

writes about cultivation throughout the year, soil conditions, and mulching, but also includes practical advice for gardens today. For instance, he instructs that the leaves of artichokes "clean pewter the best of anything." Randolph lists and discusses a number of plants that were grown in his garden including cauliflower, a large variety of peas, and several kinds of lettuces. About cauliflower, he advises that "when your Cauliflowers begin to flower, the inner leaves should be broke over them, otherwise the sun will soil their snowy colour." The best way to preserve peas, Randolph states, is "by laying them in different layers of salt, in their pods, and kept quite close."

One of the sources for how colonial cooks used garden harvests is Hannah Glasse's "Directions concerning Garden Things" in *The Art of Cookery Made Plain and Easy,* first published in 1747. George Washington, Thomas Jefferson, and Benjamin Franklin all owned copies. Glasse cautioned that "most people spoil garden things by over-boiling them. All things green should have a little crispness, for if they are over-boiled, they neither have any sweetness or beauty"—always good advice.

The John Blair House garden, a block west of The Colonial Garden, contains flowers and herbs valued by colonists for their aromatic, medicinal, and culinary properties. You will know as soon as you enter that it was designed as a fragrance garden. In colonial times, lavender, violets, and roses, along with sage and pinks, were used to scent perfumes, pomades, water, vinegar, and ammonia.

Early cookbooks, such as Eliza Smith's *The Compleat Housewife; or, Accomplish'd Gentlewoman's COMPANION,* included recipes for "sweet bags," or sachets, "burning perfumes," or incense, and potpourri. Because of its refreshing scent and insect-repellant properties, lavender was often used when making sweet bags for linens. Plants found in early potpourri recipes, such as sweet marjoram, rosemary, mint myrtle, angelica root, and orrisroot, grow in various Williamsburg gardens. Orrisroot, the dried

rhizome of an iris species, is particularly effective in fixing the scent of floral mixtures in modern potpourri recipes as well (see pages 191–192).

Many other gardens in the Historic Area contain hidden treasures. Have you ever seen pollarded sycamore trees? You will discover them behind the Taliaferro-Cole House and behind Market Square Tavern. Have you ever stood beside a corkscrew-shaped boxwood or rested under an aerial hedge? You will find these treasures in the Orlando Jones House garden. Do not miss the pleached arbors of American beech trees behind the Palace, the American hornbeam arbor behind the George Wythe House, another in the David Morton House garden covered with muscadine grapes, or one at the Colonial Nursery covered with hops. All furnish welcome shade.

You will see cordoned pear and apple trees in the Palace fruit garden. Intriguing topiaries are scattered throughout the Historic Area, especially in the Palace gardens and next to Christiana Campbell's

Above and opposite: Two popular attractions are the pleached arbor at the Palace and the fragrance garden beside the John Blair House.

Double-cordoned fruit trees *(above)* and a topiary *(opposite)* are focal points in the gardens at the Palace and Campbell's Tavern.

Tavern. You will notice how vegetables, herbs, and flowers are interplanted in the utilitarian gardens behind King's Arms and Shields Taverns. You will discover that the landscaping at the Palace includes a formal pleasure garden, a kitchen garden, a large fruit garden, a maze, a canal, and restful shaded areas. Gazebos in the gardens of The Blue Bell and the Benjamin Waller House will delight you.

When you stroll down the streets, you will enjoy the many pleasure gardens and orchards tucked behind homes just as those who live and work at Colonial Williamsburg do. A long-time resident wrote many years ago that "the presence of the gardens continues to be one of the great joys of Williamsburg. No one who lives here can raise his eyes without a glimpse of some green vista, some pattern of shrubbery or flowering tree or borders in bloom . . . gardens and the broad greens fill . . . the Historic Area, and in all seasons and all weathers make the city a sanctuary, a twentieth-century version of the green country town that was an eighteenth-century ideal."

The town is still a sanctuary today. The gardens will always provide a welcome refuge to any garden lover who cultivates, as John Custis had in 1725, "a pretty little garden in which I take more satisfaction than in anything in this world." The gardens will enhance your visit to Colonial Williamsburg and inspire new ideas for your garden and home.

Seasonal Garden Ideas

TULIPOMANIA

Tulipomania, a craze for tulips that started with Dutch scholars and collectors, reached its height in Holland between 1634 and 1637. A single bulb could command prices well in excess of the cost of a large house on one of Amsterdam's grand canals.

This phenomenon brought a great increase in botanical painting, especially those works that featured the prized flower. Botanical books with detailed drawings and paintings of tulips, and textiles and ceramic tiles with tulip motifs became widely available.

Later, when William of Orange came from Holland to England to become its king, he and his wife, Queen Mary, introduced Dutch landscaping practices, including the love of the tulip, to English gardens. These influences can be seen in Williamsburg's gardens, especially those at the Governor's Palace.

Tulipomania was the theme in several Colonial Williamsburg guesthouses open for Historic Garden Week in Virginia. Tulips displayed on fabrics and illustrated in books, paintings, and drawings were evident in the main rooms. And, of course, tulips themselves were arranged in a variety of traditional and nontraditional containers.

Whether you succumb, like our ancestors, to tulipomania, an abundance of ideas for using tulips

Brightly colored tulip material is used for the bed hangings and stool in the David Morton House. The design came from a late eighteenth-century botanical engraving by Robert John Thornton, which appeared as an illustration in his *The Temple of Flora*.

The contents in the delft bowl below an engraving of variegated tulips from *The Temple of Flora* echo specimens in the print. The desk chair seat is upholstered in the same fabric featured on page 11.

A redware multihandled drinking cup, or tyg, makes an appealing container for the saucy orange tulips on the mantel.

follows. All are inspired by the gardens in Williamsburg where tulips ranging from the tiny species variety in the side garden of the Pasteur & Galt Apothecary Shop to the magnificent and stately rows of Red Emperors at the Palace are found each spring.

Unusual delft flower bowls, wall pockets, and finger vases as well as colonial wine bottles, salt-glazed containers, and a multihandled drinking cup make excellent containers for flowers. Tulips of different colors arranged with other spring garden flowers result in colorful and often unexpected combinations.

Tulips in various forms and colors and anemones fill a delft wall pocket.

ROASTED SWEET RED PEPPER AND TOMATO SOUP

6 to 8 servings

1 can (28 ounces) whole Italian plum tomatoes

$^1/_2$ teaspoon thyme

4 tablespoons olive oil, divided

3 large carrots, peeled and chopped

2 large shallots, peeled and chopped

3 cloves garlic, peeled and chopped

4 cups chicken stock

1 ripe pear, cored, peeled, and chopped

8 large sweet red peppers

salt

cayenne

Drain, halve, and seed the tomatoes, and put them, cut side up, on an oiled foil-lined baking sheet. Sprinkle with thyme and 2 tablespoons of olive oil. Bake at 300°F. for 1 hour or until they have dried slightly. Remove them from the oven and cool. This step can be done ahead. In a large frying pan, combine the remaining oil, carrots, and shallots and sauté for 15 minutes, stirring occasionally over medium heat without browning the vegetables. Add the garlic and continue cooking for 2 minutes more. Add the chicken stock and pear and simmer for 20 to 30 min-

utes. Cool. While the vegetables are cooking, prick the peppers and place them on a rack 2 inches from the broiler and turn as they become charred. When all sides are blackened, remove and place them in a plastic bag for 10 minutes to make it easier to remove the skins. Take them out of the bag, cut off the tops, and remove the ribs, seeds, and skins. Cut into pieces. Add the tomatoes and peppers to the vegetable mixture and puree in small batches in a food processor. Put the soup through a sieve to remove any seeds. Add salt and cayenne to taste. **Note:** Serve hot or cold, garnished with chopped yellow peppers, sour cream or yogurt, and chopped cilantro.

Finger vases, used in the eighteenth century, are still popular in Williamsburg.

W. TARLTON

A colorful black, white, and red luncheon table awaits guests in the George Reid House. Red and white tulips unexpectedly combined with anemones and ranunculus, red napkins tied with black ribbons and sealing wax stamps, and black-and-white checked place mats pick up the colors in the sign over the mantel.

A spring garden using native plant materials has been created on a mantel in the George Reid House. Its colors repeat those of the Carolina parakeet and red-winged blackbird above. Mark Catesby, a colonial naturalist and artist who lived in Williamsburg for seven years and gathered specimens for an illustrated natural history, drew them.

How to Make a Spring Garden for a Mantel

Supplies and materials needed: Narrow floral container or a chicken feeder with the top bar removed, instant deluxe floral foam, floral preservative, galax leaves, Alexandrian laurel, boxwood, flowers, and other conditioned plant materials (see page 206), and spring flowers of different colors, shapes, and textures.

If you use a chicken feeder, paint it the color of your mantel or dark green. Cut the floral foam to fit about 1/2 inch above the top of your container and soak it in water with floral preservative. Place the foam in the container. Insert the galax leaves and Alexandrian laurel or other foliage in the foam around the front and sides to conceal the container. Insert a few sprigs of boxwood to give the effect of a thicker garden.

Place an assortment of the taller blossoms such as columbine, miniature daffodils, yellow and red parrot tulips, and paper-white narcissus at the back of the container. Place shorter paper-white narcissus, tulips, daffodils, anemones, and scilla in front.

Vary the height, textures, colors, and the direction of the flowers' faces to give the garden a natural appearance. **Note:** This type of garden can be made at any time of the year following these basic instructions and used anywhere you need to place a long and narrow arrangement.

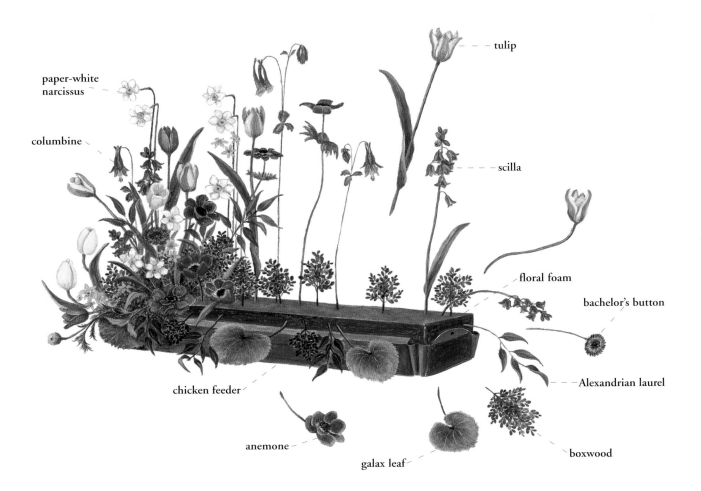

paper-white narcissus

columbine

tulip

scilla

floral foam

bachelor's button

Alexandrian laurel

chicken feeder

anemone

galax leaf

boxwood

Here is tulipomania on a small scale in this centerpiece featuring a collection of miniature furniture and accessories, and tulips. What fun it is to share whatever you collect with friends by using your treasures in a special table setting.

This setting includes a one-inch-high finger vase filled with minute yet botanically correct red and yellow tulips *(below)* that replicates the full-size one on the sideboard *(above)*. These miniature delft plates were copied from the original ones on the table *(above)*.

During the annual Colonial Williamsburg Garden Symposium, a group of gardeners have been invited to luncheon at the Bracken Tenement. The centerpiece, a miniature version of the gazebo at The Blue Bell, sits in its own diminutive garden.

EASTER IDEAS

Many objects can be adapted to be used with flowers. A handsome pair of Easter bunnies *(above)* sporting packs spilling over with spring blossoms watch over a nest of candy eggs, tiny baskets filled with Jordan almonds, and lemon tarts decorated with fresh pansies.

These pottery containers are not watertight. To use them, form a nosegay or a circular arrangement of blossoms. Cut the stems about three inches long, wrap in a wet, folded paper towel and then in plastic wrap, and place into the packs. Make sure to conceal the plastic wrap. This wooden cherub *(left)* becomes a container for flowers by first lining the shell with plastic wrap. Then place a piece of wet floral foam on the plastic to fit about two inches high. Circle the foam with small sprigs of boxwood and, using a skewer, make holes in it to hold the delicate stems of the pansies.

EASTER CAKE WITH STRAWBERRY AND LEMON FILLING

3/4 cup unsalted butter
1 1/2 cups sugar, divided
3 cups cake flour, sifted
1 teaspoon salt
4 teaspoons baking powder
1 cup milk
1 teaspoon vanilla extract
1 teaspoon lemon extract
1 tablespoon lemon zest
5 egg whites
1 pound fresh strawberries
1 cup heavy whipping cream
2 tablespoons confectioners' sugar

Preheat the oven to 350°F. Grease well and lightly flour the bottom and sides of two 8-inch round cake pans. Line the bottom of each pan with a circle of waxed paper. Cream the butter and all but 5 tablespoons sugar until light and fluffy. Sift the cake flour, salt, and baking powder together. Add the dry ingredients and milk alternately, beating constantly. Add the vanilla and lemon extracts, and lemon zest. Beat the egg whites until stiff peaks form. Beat in the remaining sugar. Fold into the batter and pour into the prepared pans. Bake at 350°F. for 25 to 30 minutes or until done. Do not overbake. Cool in the pans for 10 minutes before turning out on racks. Wash and dry the strawberries and remove their stems. Use a knife to cut the berries into small pieces, retaining as much of the juice as possible. Cut each layer in half. Spread one-third of the filling and one-third of the berries over the bottom layer. Repeat for the second and third layers. Whip the cream until soft peaks form, then add the confectioners' sugar and beat until stiff. Place the remaining layer on top with the inside facing up and ice the cake with the whipped cream.

LEMON FILLING

3/4 cup sugar
4 tablespoons lemon juice
1 tablespoon lemon zest
1/4 cup butter
3 eggs, well beaten
1 egg white

Mix the sugar, juice, and zest. Melt the butter in the top of a double boiler. Add the sugar mixture and eggs. Continue cooking over hot water until very thick, stirring constantly. Cool. Beat the egg white until stiff peaks form and then fold into the custard. Cover the custard with plastic wrap and refrigerate until ready to use.

21

A delicious lemon tart, garnished with mint, is decorated with a fresh pansy under a wine glaze.

LEMON TARTS WITH GLAZED PANSIES
12 small tarts

1³/4 cups vanilla sugar
6 to 8 tablespoons lemon juice
2 tablespoons lemon zest
1/2 cup butter
6 eggs, well beaten
12 small baked tart shells

Insert a vanilla bean in the sugar in a closed jar and let it sit for at least a week to make the vanilla sugar. Mix the sugar, juice, and zest. Melt the butter in the top of a double boiler. Add the sugar mixture and eggs. Continue cooking over hot water until very thick, stirring constantly. Cool, cover, and refrigerate. Fill the tart shells when chilled. Decorate each tart with a fresh pansy under a gelatin wine glaze (see page 36).

The choice of the container for the Easter eggs *(opposite)* was inspired by the whitewashed fences that enclose many of Williamsburg's gardens.

How to Make Silk Pansies

Supplies and materials needed: 5 x 3/8 inch silk ribbon for each pansy, marking pencil, thread, #9 milliner's needle, small, sharp scissors, 1 x 1 inch crinoline for each pansy, yellow embroidery thread, and 1 x 3/8 inch green silk ribbon for each leaf (optional).

Take a 5-inch piece of ribbon and mark light lines at 1-inch intervals.

Double a piece of thread 12 inches long, knot it, and, starting at one end, take small stitches to gather the ribbon as shown. Pull the gathers as you stitch. The stitches go on either side of the pencil marks.

After sewing and forming the petals, check to see that petals 1 to 4 are tightly gathered. Petal 5 should be looser. Knot and cut the thread.

Place petals 1 and 2 on the crinoline. With knotted thread, secure the gathered edge of petal 1 to the crinoline with one or two tiny stitches. Repeat with petal 2. Fold petals 3 and 4 back over petals 1 and 2. Tack petal 3 on top of and slightly lower than petal 2, using the same tiny tack stitch at the gathering line into the crinoline. Repeat with petal 4.

Bring petal 5 up so the gathering line joins petals 3 and 4, securing petal 5 to the crinoline touching petals 3 and 4 to close any opening. Add tiny, yellow French knots to make a center for the pansy. Trim the crinoline so it does not show yet supports the pansy where it is stitched.

To make a leaf, take a 1-inch piece of green ribbon and follow the diagram, gathering the long edge and, pulling the gathers together, knot. Tuck the leaf under the pansy and stitch it onto the crinoline.

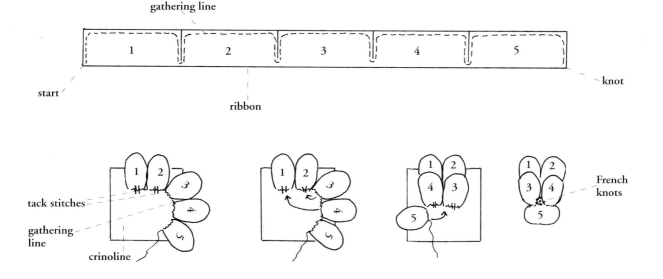

How To Make a Floral-Decorated Hoop

Children still play with hoops as they run down Colonial Williamsburg's garden paths. Here the hoop has been transformed into a hanging decoration for an Easter garden setting. Two embroidery hoops are fastened together and decorated with fresh flowers.

Supplies and materials needed: Two 10-inch wooden embroidery hoops, green floral tape, #26 gauge spool wire, #18 gauge green floral wire, wire cutters, conditioned plant materials (see page 206), plant mister, and ribbon.

Wrap each hoop with green floral tape, which will help hold the plant material in place. The tape also obscures the color of the wood.

Insert one hoop inside the other at a right angle to divide the hoops equally. Secure the top and bottom crossing points with spool wire. Make a loop with floral wire at the top for a hanger.

Assemble the plant materials (2- to 3-inch sprigs of boxwood with their lower leaves removed, pansies, Johnny-jump-ups, and a mixture of other spring flowers are used here) and stand them in water.

Combine two or three pieces of foliage and one or two flowers and wrap the stem ends with several twists of the spool wire. Keep the bunches standing in water as you make them. Make approximately forty

3-inch bunches of foliage and flowers for the outside of the hoops. Make forty bunches of foliage without flowers for the insides. Mist the bunches well, put the container into a plastic bag, and refrigerate. Depending on the plant materials, you may make these bunches the day before or several hours ahead.

To assemble, start at the bottom of one of the hoops. Hold a bunch containing the flowers on the outside and one with plain foliage on the inside with the cut ends facing the top of the form. Secure the two bunches to the form by wrapping the floral tape around the stem ends of the two bunches with the hoop between. Continue wrapping two bunches at a time onto the hoops, overlapping the previous stem ends and working toward the top. As you attach the bunches to the hoops, vary the colors and types of flowers to achieve a pleasing balance.

When completed, cut the ribbon and add it to the top and bottom. Mist well and frequently.

Note: For another decorating idea using embroidery hoops, see page 110.

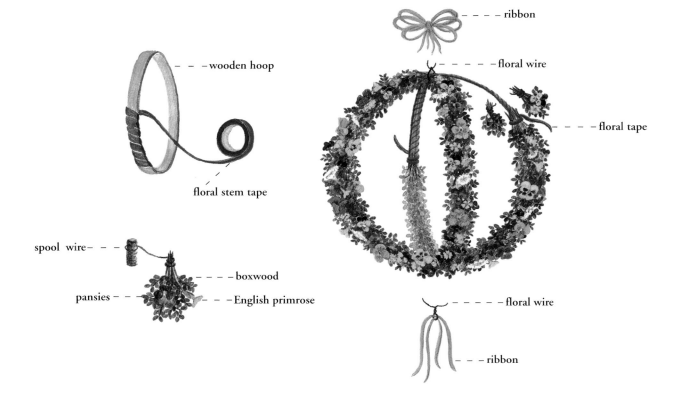

– – –wooden hoop

floral stem tape

spool wire– – –

pansies – –

– – –boxwood

– –English primrose

– – – ribbon

– – – – – floral wire

– – – – –floral tape

– – – – – floral wire

– – – ribbon

DRAPERS' DINNER AT THE COLLEGE OF WILLIAM AND MARY

The Drapers' Company, one of the guilds organized in London during the Middle Ages, was formally chartered in 1364 by woolen cloth merchants. Today, it is a charitable foundation with long ties to the College of William and Mary. As its gift to the college during its tercentenary celebration in 1993, the Drapers' provided for the permanent endowment of an exchange scholarship between law students from William and Mary and Queen Mary College of the University of London.

A profusion of spring garden blooms creates a magnificent and colorful array reminiscent of an English country house party in an American setting. At a formal dinner at the President's House, visiting members of the Drapers' Company are honored. Selected to reflect the colors in the Imari china, the flowers are arranged on silver salvers at each end of the table and cascade from a footed dish in the center. Eggcups at each lady's place hold individual arrangements.

Yellow daffodils, jonquils, yellow, salmon, and red ranunculus, and other spring flowers spill out of a large, eighteenth-century silver epergne in the shape of a Chinese pagoda.

The large arrangement of mixed spring flowers below portraits of King William and Queen Mary in the entry hall prepares guests for the spectacular array of colors awaiting them in the dining room.

The table is set for the distinguished representatives of the Drapers' Company from London.

OLD FORMS, NEW WAYS
TOPIARIES

Examples of boxwood and yaupon topiaries are found in many Williamsburg gardens. This ancient horticultural art was passed down from Roman times and became popular in European and English gardens in the seventeenth and early eighteenth centuries. The Virginia colonists, remembering these devices from England, filled the first Williamsburg gardens with them.

Portable topiaries are popular today and easy to maintain. They can be enjoyed indoors during cold weather and easily moved outside into semishaded areas when it becomes warmer.

A topiary planted by Colonial Williamsburg is ringed with a bed of pink flowers.

A circular-shaped, large-leafed portable ivy topiary is on a table in the Chiswell-Bucktrout House garden. Examples of clipped boxwood topiaries planted in the garden are visible.

An old basket filled with pansies and other spring flowers and a heart-shaped rosemary topiary have been placed on the well behind Market Square Tavern.

Classic rosemary topiaries, a ball and a circle shape, sit on a fence behind the Chiswell-Bucktrout House.

Also displayed in the Chiswell-Bucktrout House garden is a topiary trained into three balls.

How to Make a Portable Topiary

Supplies and material needed: Pebbles, container, potting soil mixed with perlite, prostrate rosemary or ivy plant with six to eight 8-inch-long tendrils, wire topiary form, raffia or other plant ties, and floral pins.

Whether you select a traditional or whimsical shape, the making of and caring for a topiary follow the same basic rules. A topiary form can be created quickly if you start with a mature plant.

Put a layer of pebbles in the container and fill it halfway with the potting soil. Plant the rosemary or ivy and fill in around the plant with potting soil, firming the soil to eliminate air pockets. Carefully insert the prongs of the topiary form into the container. Twine the stems around the base of the rod that connects with the ball. Remove the leaves as you twine, always keeping about 40 percent of the foliage at the ends to nourish the plant.

As each piece is twisted around the wire, temporarily secure it with a tie. Once all the stems are twisted around the rod and the wire area is covered, tie all the stems together where they join the ball with a plant tie and remove the temporary ties. Continue to interweave the long tendrils around the frame and tie as needed as the plant grows. Anchor the ends by tucking them under the parts of the form that have not been covered.

You can add flowers to circular and ball-shaped topiaries to make special decorations. Chamomile blossoms and sprigs of candytuft have been added to this circular form to make a fresh decoration for an informal gathering.

Also used is an unusual wire frame particularly suited to the long tendrils of many varieties of small-leafed ivy. Two plants can be used on this form.

It is started in the same way. Twine one or more of the longest tendrils around the supporting wire and secure every few inches. Continue to twine up and around the top left curve. Loosely tie the ends of the tendril or tendrils to the frame. Repeat this process with one or more of the remaining long tendrils on the upper right curve. As the ivy grows, twist the new growth around the form and tie it. Pinch off the ends when they grow beyond the curl of the wire.

Repeat this process for the two lower curves of the form.

Let the shortest tendrils cascade over the sides of the container. As they grow, tendrils can help fill in the form. Using floral pins, distribute tendrils around the container so the topiary is balanced.

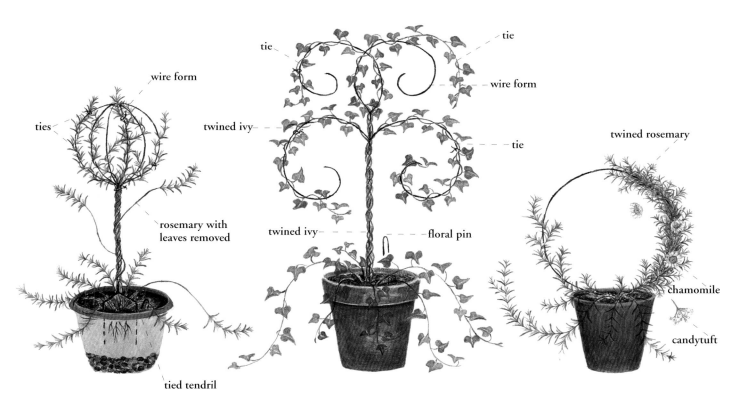

EDIBLE FLOWERS: GARNISHES FROM THE GARDEN

Pleasing the palate and the eye are goals when using edible flowers and foliage. A garden yielding edible flowers throughout the seasons will give you the materials to create many eye-appealing dishes. For instance, if you sprinkle fresh mixed greens with nasturtiums, both blossoms and leaves, yellow calendula petals, and whole blooms from sage, the result will be a salad of sensational colors *(above)*. Dressed with a classic vinaigrette, it is a feast for the palate. The other goal is to have these flowers planted close to your kitchen door!

In early spring, Johnny-jump-ups, pansies, violets, and calendula petals provide dramatic colors and forms for decorating a variety of foods. Later, daylilies, fairy roses, borage, the petals of Lemon Gem marigolds, and chive blossoms can be used. In the early fall, pineapple sage blooms not only brighten, but also add a subtle taste to, dishes they accent.

Cut the flowers in the morning after the dew has evaporated. Swish them gently in a bowl of cool water and pat dry. If you are not using them immediately, place the stems in a dish of water or between layers of damp paper towels.

As with herbs, some flowers taste best with certain foods. Daylilies are sweet and have a crisp texture and a taste that serves as a nice complement to pasta when slivered and dressed with lemon thyme, olive oil, and lemon juice. The striking red florets of bee balm are delicious with fruits, cakes, and ice creams.

It is important to learn which plants are edible. Some that are not particularly tasty, yet are not poisonous, can serve as garnishes. Do not use any plant material on food unless you know it is nontoxic.

Know the source of your flowers. Florist flowers have usually been heavily fertilized and sprayed to produce beautiful blooms for show, but not to eat. Even if you are certain that the flowers you select are edible, it is best to use just the petals because stamens and pistils of flowers such as marigolds and tulips can cause reactions in people allergic to pollens.

What better place to find a hedgehog than in a garden of Johnny-jump-ups? According to English folklore, it is a sign of good luck to find a hedgehog in your garden. Hedgehogs made from marzipan were used on eighteenth-century dining tables. A modern adaptation made with two cheeses and sherry is popular at Christmas. This version calls for port, a wine traditionally served in England at the end of a meal. Use seasonal materials from your garden, such as scented geraniums in summer, washed and dried leaves and acorns in fall, or kale in winter, to display this happy little fellow.

Opposite: Spicy carrot slices simmered in orange juice and white wine until tender yet still crisp are garnished with mint sprigs and garlic chive florets and thyme blossoms.

CHESHIRE CHEESE HEDGEHOG

12 ounces cream cheese
4 cups Cheshire cheese, grated
$^1/_3$ cup port
1 teaspoon curry powder
$^1/_2$ teaspoon dry mustard
$^1/_2$ teaspoon salt
$^1/_4$ teaspoon cayenne
currants
nutmeg
2 cups slivered almonds, toasted

Place the cheeses, port, curry powder, dry mustard, salt, and cayenne in a food processor and combine well. Chill for several hours. Form a mound for the body with three-fourths of the mixture. Model the face and ears from the remaining mixture and join to the body. Use currants for the eyes. Color the face and ears with a shake of nutmeg. Insert slivered almonds for the spines. Chill.

FLORAL-DECORATED CHEESES WITH GELATIN WINE GLAZE

The top of a small Brie is decorated with a large pansy encircled by smaller violas edged with dill sprigs and surrounded with white Ophelia begonias and more yellow pansies. A large purple pansy ringed with tiny violet leaves and thyme sprigs is centered on a small Camembert on a bed of large violet leaves. Woodruff whorls and other herbs are pressed into the sides of the cheese. Both cheeses are coated with a gelatin wine glaze that keeps the flowers fresh looking and appetizing.

GELATIN WINE GLAZE

Brie or Camembert cheese
edible flowers and herbs such as Johnny-jump-ups,
    pansies, violets, dill, mint, and thyme
1 teaspoon unflavored gelatin
1 cup dry white wine

Place the cheese on a cake rack over a dish. Rinse the flowers and herbs and very gently pat them dry. Next,

dissolve the gelatin in the wine over low heat. Remove from the heat. Place the pan in a bowl of ice and water. Stir very slowly until the mixture thickens slightly but is still liquid. Spoon the glaze over the cheese. Refrigerate for 3 to 4 minutes. Carefully arrange the plant materials on the cheese and refrigerate for 15 minutes. Remove the cheese, reheat and spoon more of the glaze over the plant materials, and return it to the refrigerator. Repeat until the plant materials are well covered. Excess glaze that accumulates on the plate can be reused. When it becomes thick, reheat the glaze until it liquefies.

PINEAPPLE UPSIDE-DOWN CAKE WITH PINEAPPLE SAGE
6 to 8 servings

3 tablespoons unsalted butter, melted
1/2 cup light brown sugar, packed
6 pineapple slices, fresh or canned, well drained
1 1/2 cups all-purpose flour
1 teaspoon salt
3/4 teaspoon baking soda
1/2 teaspoon cinnamon
1/4 teaspoon ground cloves
1/2 cup butter, softened
1/2 cup granulated sugar
1/2 cup molasses
1 egg, lightly beaten
1 1/2 tablespoons fresh ginger, minced, or 1/2 teaspoon dried ginger
2 teaspoons pineapple sage, minced
1/2 cup boiling water
1 cup whipping cream
1 to 1 1/2 tablespoons candied ginger, minced
pineapple sage sprig

Preheat the oven to 350°F. Pour the unsalted butter into a 10-inch round cake pan and stir in the brown sugar. Place the pineapple slices in a single layer on top of the brown sugar. Combine the flour, salt, bak-

ing soda, cinnamon, and cloves in a medium bowl and set aside. Cream the softened butter and granulated sugar until light and fluffy. Add the molasses, egg, ginger, and pineapple sage and beat until smooth. Add the flour mixture and the boiling water, one-third at a time, and mix well. Pour the batter over the pineapple slices and bake at 350°F. for 45 to 50 minutes. Invert the cake onto a serving plate and rest the pan over the cake for 1 to 2 minutes to allow the syrup to drain onto the top. Whip the cream until soft peaks form, add the candied ginger, and whip until stiff peaks form. Serve warm topped with whipped cream and garnished with a sprig of pineapple sage.

In the early fall, pineapple sage is used to flavor and garnish pineapple upside-down cake. Behind the dessert is a bouquet of pineapple sage.

DESSERT IN THE
BENJAMIN WALLER HOUSE GAZEBO

Spring in Williamsburg is particularly picturesque in this garden with its charming gazebo. The sparkling blossoms of a white dogwood tree spill over into the garden behind the Benjamin Waller House. Miss Luty Blow traced the garden's design drawn by her grandmother, Eliza Waller. Her tracing was followed when Colonial Williamsburg restored the garden. Clipped boxwood edge the beds filled with spring bulbs and variegated foliage.

A dessert is laid on a pink organdy cloth. Edible flowers decorate the cake, iced in a basket-weave pattern, and the tiny petits fours. Sugared fruits, tulips filled with strawberry mousse, and pastillage baskets (*opposite, above,* and page 40) containing candied violets, mints, and Jordan almonds, complete the picture. The pastillage baskets are made of a mixture of sugar, gelatin, and water.

How to Candy Edible Flowers and Flower Petals

Supplies and materials needed: Edible petals and flowers *(opposite)*, 2 teaspoons powdered egg whites, 2 teaspoons water, wire whip, tweezers, artist's brush, superfine sugar, and cookie rack.

Collect petals and flowers that have not been sprayed with fungicides or insecticides. Pansies, violets, and rose petals are good choices. Remove the stamens and pistils of the larger flowers. Rinse the plant materials and allow them to air dry on paper towels.

Mix 2 teaspoons powdered egg whites and 2 teaspoons water using a wire whip. Allow the egg whites to dissolve and absorb the water, then beat vigorously with the whip until foamy.

Hold the blossom or petal with tweezers and evenly coat both sides with the beaten egg whites using a soft artist's brush so both surfaces are evenly coated. The sugar will only adhere to areas coated with egg white. Gently sprinkle the petals or flowers with sugar as soon as they are coated with egg whites. Shake off any excess sugar. Place on a cookie rack to dry. Most will dry overnight in a nonhumid location and then can be stored in an air-tight container. Some whole flowers will take a day or more to dry.

A pastillage, or sugar, box, given by a spring bride as a keepsake, is decorated with sugared pansies. The decorations are held in place with royal icing.

EDIBLE FLOWERS AND HERBS

The following blossoms and petals from common flowers and herbs are easy to grow. Most are found in the gardens of Colonial Williamsburg, and are used to garnish foods, in cooking, or for candied decoration. Remove the stamens and pistils from the daylily, squash, and tulip blossoms.

basil blossoms	*mustard blossoms*
borage blossoms	*nasturtium blossoms*
calendula petals	*oregano blossoms*
chive blossoms	*pansy blossoms*
daylily blossoms	*pineapple sage blossoms*
dianthus blossoms	*rose petals*
lavender blossoms	*sage blossoms*
Lemon Gem marigold	*squash blossoms*
petals	*thyme blossoms*
lemon verbena blossoms	*tuberous begonia blossoms*
marjoram blossoms	*tulip petals*
monarda blossoms	*violet blossoms*

FRESH STRAWBERRY MOUSSE
10 to 12 servings

16 ounces strawberries, washed, stems removed,
  and divided
1/2 cup sugar
1 cup water
2 tablespoons strawberry-flavored gelatin
1 1/2 teaspoons unflavored gelatin
1 pint whipping cream
10 to 12 tulip blossoms
10 to 12 meringues (see page 161)
10 to 12 mint sprigs

Cut all but one or two strawberries in quarters, place in a food processor, and puree. Strain through a fine sieve. Mix the strawberries and sugar and set aside. Bring the water to a boil, add the strawberry-flavored and unflavored gelatins, and stir until they have dis-solved. Remove from the heat and let cool. Add the gelatin mixture to the strawberries and sugar and let thicken slightly. Whip the cream until soft peaks form and fold into the mixture. Cover and chill several hours or overnight. Gently rinse and dry the tulip blossoms. Place a meringue ring on each plate. Remove the tulip stems and carefully cut out the pistils and stamens with small scissors so the insides of the blooms are empty. Immediately place the tulips into the rings and gently fill them with the mousse. Garnish each with a thin slice of strawberry and a mint sprig.

Tulips with their pistils and stamens removed have been filled with strawberry mousse. Decorated with an English daisy from the garden and a slice of berry, the tulips are served in small meringue rings.

BERRIES GALORE

Nothing says summer as much as fresh berries from the garden. Juicy and luscious blackberries, raspberries, and blueberries, and glistening ripe strawberries all tempt the palate.

A dessert table is set up behind Providence Hall House, one of Colonial Williamsburg's eighteenth-century guesthouses located on the Golden Horseshoe Golf Course. Across a fairway, a row of hot pink crape myrtles announce that summer has arrived in Williamsburg.

The colorful centerpiece of spiraling fresh berries nestled on a moss-covered cone is outlined against the pink blooms of the trees. Cinnamon sticks serve as a trunk for this "faux" topiary. Icy cold raspberry lemonade, English cream tarts topped with fresh berries, and a delectable mix of fragrant berries offer a sweet respite from the warmth of the summer afternoon.

How to Make a "Faux" Topiary Using a Styrofoam Cone

Supplies and materials needed: Styrofoam cone form approximately 10 x 4 inches, glue (compatible with Styrofoam), five or six 8-inch cinnamon sticks, sheet moss, floral pins or 2-inch pieces of #18 gauge green floral wire, decorative container, plastic liner or pot that will fit into outer container, masking tape, plaster of paris, paint stirrer, gravel, assorted fresh berries, and wooden toothpicks.

Cut off the top inch of the cone. Cut a small hole about 2 inches deep in the center of the base. Put a generous amount of glue in the hole. Take the cinnamon sticks, coat their ends with glue, and push them into the hole. Keep the form vertical. Allow the glue to dry. Attach the sheet moss to the cone using pins or pieces of floral wire bent into hairpin shapes. Completely cover the cone.

Select a decorative container and a plastic liner or pot that will fit inside it. Tape over any drainage holes with masking tape. Fill almost to the top with plaster of paris. Add water and stir quickly. Add more water or plaster of paris as needed and thoroughly mix the ingredients until the plaster is smooth and thick. Insert the trunk of the cone formed from the bunch of cinnamon sticks, checking that it is centered and vertical. Let the plaster of paris dry for 24 hours, then place the liner in the outside container. Fill any remaining space with gravel to give the topiary weight and stability.

If the topiary tips to one side either before or after it is decorated, carefully lift the whole form in its liner out of the gravel, pour the gravel into another container, and start the process again by returning the topiary form and liner to the container and surrounding it with gravel. Do not try to straighten it. It is better to start over.

Select the berries and a design: spiral, diagonal, horizontal, or one that covers all the form. Insert a line of toothpicks into the form to establish your pattern and impale the first row of berries onto the toothpicks. Each of the succeeding rows should be parallel to this row, spaced more closely at the top. Impale each strawberry onto two toothpicks to hold them securely. Cut the toothpicks near the top of the cone in half. Select a beautifully shaped large berry for the top of the cone. When the topiary is complete, cover the gravel with sheet moss. **Note:** For attractive green moss, see the conditioning section (page 207).

remove top

floral pins

Styrofoam cone

sheet moss to cover cone

cinnamon sticks

plaster of paris

plastic liner

strawberry

blackberry

toothpicks

raspberry

decorative container

blueberry

gravel

ENGLISH CREAM TARTS WITH FRESH BERRIES
8 regular or 2 dozen small tarts

1/2 cup sugar
3 tablespoons cornstarch
5 egg yolks
2 cups milk
1/2 vanilla bean, split lengthwise
1/4 cup unsalted butter
1 tablespoon kirsch
8 4-inch or 24 1 1/2-inch baked tart shells
fresh blackberries
fresh raspberries
fresh blueberries

Combine the sugar and cornstarch. Add the egg yolks. Beat well. Place the milk and vanilla bean in a saucepan and scald. Remove the bean from the milk. Gradually pour the milk over the egg mixture, beating constantly. Bring the mixture almost to a boil and cook, stirring constantly, for 2 minutes. Remove it from the heat. Stir the butter and kirsch into the custard and let it cool. Place a sheet of plastic wrap on the surface of the custard and chill it thoroughly. Fill the baked tart shells with the custard and top one-third with blackberries, one-third with raspberries, and the rest with blueberries.

RASPBERRY LEMONADE
8 to 10 servings

1 1/2 cups raspberries
1 1/4 cups sugar
2 cups lemon juice
5 cups cold water

Mash the raspberries and sugar with a wooden spoon and allow the mixture to sit for 20 minutes. Combine with the lemon juice and press it through a sieve into a 2-quart bowl. Pour the water into the bowl through the remaining pulp in the sieve to extract all possible sweetness and flavor from the berries. Chill and add ice before serving.

FROZEN BLACKBERRY APRICOT MOUSSE
12 servings

1 tablespoon unflavored gelatin
1 tablespoon cold water
1 tablespoon orange zest and juice from 1 large orange
2 pints fresh blackberries, divided
6 fresh apricots, peeled and sliced
2 eggs
1/3 cup sugar
2 tablespoons plus 1 teaspoon cassis
1/2 teaspoon cinnamon
1/8 teaspoon salt
1 1/2 cups whipping cream
sprigs of mint

Soak the gelatin in the cold water for 5 minutes. Add the orange juice and zest, all but twelve blackberries, and the apricots. Bring the fruit mixture just to a boil, stirring constantly. Cool it to room temperature. Place the fruit mixture in a food processor and puree it, then strain it through a sieve. Beat the eggs until they are light and fluffy, then beat in the sugar gradually. Combine the egg mixture with the fruit mixture, 2 tablespoons of cassis, cinnamon, and salt. Whip 1 cup of the cream until stiff and fold it into the mixture. Freeze the mousse until it is firm. Transfer the mousse from the freezer to the refrigerator 2 hours before serving, then take it out of the refrigerator 30 to 45 minutes before serving. Whip the remaining cream until soft peaks form, add 1 teaspoon of cassis, and whip until stiff peaks form. Top each dessert with a dollop of cream garnished with a blackberry and a sprig of mint.

SUMMER LUNCHEON

In a secluded garden behind Christiana Campbell's Tavern, a large poached salmon is ringed with lime slices and blackberries. The variegated foliage of Solomon's seal, the white roses and lisianthus blossoms, and the green maidenhair fern, Alexandrian laurel, hellebore, and boxwood foliage look cool on this hot summer day. Many of these same flowers and foliage are found on the cloth, which is reproduced from an eighteenth-century copperplate-printed fabric in Colonial Williamsburg's collections.

POACHED SALMON

6 to 8 servings

1/2 cup onion, chopped
1 tablespoon butter
1 heaping cup celery, chopped
1 heaping cup carrots, chopped
1 5- to 6- pound whole salmon, cleaned and scaled
  before weighing
1 lemon, sliced
2 bunches parsley
3 1/2 cups white zinfandel wine
2 bay leaves
6 peppercorns
3 cloves
1/2 cup mayonnaise
juice of 1 lemon
2 tablespoons minced dill
baby green and red lettuces
limes, sliced
blackberries

Sauté the onions in the butter, then add the celery and carrots and simmer for 30 minutes; cool. Fill the cavity of the salmon with lemon slices and one-half of 1 bunch of parsley and wrap it in cheesecloth rinsed in cold water. Place the salmon on the greased rack of a fish poacher. Pour the wine over the salmon and add the vegetables around it. Add enough cold water to come slightly more than halfway over the salmon. Add the bay leaves, peppercorns, cloves, and 1 bunch of parsley. Bring the liquid to a boil and immediately reduce it to a simmer. Cook the salmon 5 to 8 minutes per pound from the time it reaches a simmer, or 10 minutes per inch at its thickest part. For example, simmer a fish measuring 3 inches thick for 30 minutes. Baste the salmon with the liquid frequently. Remove the salmon and drain. Allow it to cool slightly. Open the cheesecloth, but do not take out the salmon. Immediately remove the skin, the thin brown sections, and the fins. Use a sharp knife to trim off the uneven area along the cavity. If the salmon will be served with its head and tail, be careful to protect them when trimming the fish. After it is trimmed, gently place the salmon on the serving platter still in the cheesecloth. Carefully turn it over, remove the cheesecloth, then the skin and dark flesh. Combine the mayonnaise and lemon juice. Select the side of the salmon that looks the best and spoon on a gelatin wine glaze (see page 36) or coat it with the mayonnaise mixture, retaining any extra mixture. Chop the rest of the parsley, add dill, and sprinkle the herbs over the salmon. Serve it with the remaining mayonnaise mixture. Surround the salmon with young green and red lettuces, ringed by a row of overlapping lime slices and blackberries. Put slices of limes over the gill area and place a blackberry on the eye of the fish.

THREE PESTOS

A colorful table is set with choices of basil, mint and spinach, and walnut-rosemary pestos from the summer bounty of the Chiswell-Bucktrout House garden. A partially hollowed out watermelon holds rudbeckia, zinnias, coreopsis, apple mint, and rosemary. The flowers are inserted into the melon's flesh and its sugar helps keep them fresh.

BASIL PESTO
6 servings

2/3 cup olive oil
2 cups basil leaves, tightly packed, stems removed
2 cups Parmesan cheese, grated and divided
3 small garlic cloves
juice of 1 lemon
1/2 teaspoon white pepper
1 cup walnuts
2 tomatoes, chopped

Place the oil into a food processor, add the basil, pulse until coarsely chopped, then puree. Add 1 cup of the cheese, the garlic, lemon juice, white pepper, and walnuts, and puree the mixture at least 1 minute. Serve the pesto with thin pasta and the remaining cheese and chopped tomatoes.

MINT AND SPINACH PESTO
4 servings

1 1/2 cups fresh mint leaves, lightly packed
20 large basil leaves, lightly packed
1/4 cup Italian parsley sprigs, lightly packed
3 tablespoons chopped spinach, cooked and minced
4 tablespoons unsalted butter, softened
2 tablespoons lemon juice
1/3 cup olive oil
1 1/2 teaspoons salt, or to taste
black pepper, freshly ground
1 cup Parmesan cheese, grated and divided

Place the mint, basil, parsley, spinach, butter, lemon juice, olive oil, salt, pepper to taste, and 1/2 cup of the grated cheese in a food processor and pulse until smooth. Serve the pesto with pasta and the remaining cheese.

WALNUT-ROSEMARY PESTO
4 servings

3/4 cup walnuts
1 1/2 tablespoons fresh rosemary, chopped
1 small garlic clove
1 tablespoon lemon zest
1/2 cup Parmesan cheese, grated
3 tablespoons olive oil
1/8 teaspoon salt
1/4 teaspoon black pepper, freshly ground
2 teaspoons lemon juice

Place the walnuts in a skillet and cook over medium heat for 5 minutes or until lightly toasted. Remove them from the pan, chop coarsely, and let cool. Add the rosemary, garlic, and lemon zest, and finely chop the mixture. Combine the walnut mixture in a small bowl with the cheese, olive oil, salt, pepper, and lemon juice. Mash the mixture with the back of a spoon. Serve the pesto with pasta. **Note:** When draining the pasta, save some of the cooking water for thinning the pesto. Add 1 tablespoon at a time to the pesto to make it the desired consistency.

TIDEWATER SEAFOOD FEAST

Chesapeake Bay blue crabs steamed with hot and spicy crab boil are a popular summer meal in Tidewater Virginia and often served with corn on the cob. Roasted sweet red pepper and tomato soup (see page 14), steamed shrimp in a large clamshell served with a bowl of black bean, red pepper, and corn salsa (see page 53), lemon wedges, and plenty of napkins are added to the menu.

Crab and corn on the cob are as indigenous to a Tidewater summer as Virginia ham and pecan pie to Christmas.

How to Make a Cone on a Nail-Studded Wooden Form Using Vegetables

Supplies and materials needed: 10-inch nail-studded wooden cone form (a 7-inch and a 10-inch cone are available through Colonial Williamsburg), 2^1/$_2$-inch (8 penny) galvanized finishing nails (optional), hammer, 8-inch heavy cardboard cake round, Spanish moss, latex gloves, different varieties, sizes, and colors of peppers, #18 gauge green floral wire, wire cutters, and plant materials for the base such as broccoli rabe and cayenne peppers.

If you use vegetables such as these peppers on a wooden cone, hammer additional finishing nails between the existing nails on the form, angling them up to better secure the peppers.

Take a cardboard cake round, wider than the base of the cone, cover it with plastic wrap, tape the wrap underneath, and place the cone on the round. Using a base wider than the cone will make the finished decoration easier to move. Cover the cone with

Elegant apple cones made on nail-studded wooden forms are the centerpiece of many a traditional Williamsburg Christmas table. The form can be adapted for other uses any time of the year. Here, a variety of colorful peppers brings fire to the table.

Spanish moss to conceal the form and help hold the pieces of floral wire used to secure smaller peppers.

Wear gloves to protect your hands while han-

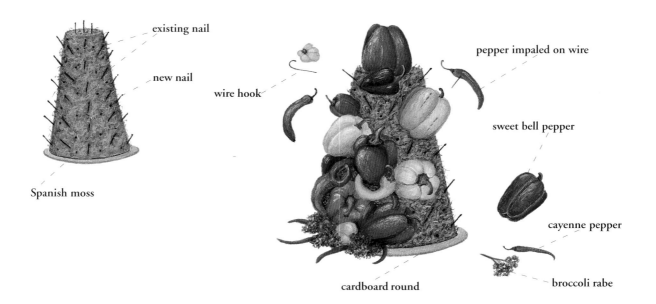

existing nail

new nail

wire hook

Spanish moss

pepper impaled on wire

sweet bell pepper

cayenne pepper

broccoli rabe

cardboard round

dling the peppers. Divide them into groups by colors and sizes. Impale the largest peppers randomly, one color at a time, saving one large, colorful, and well-shaped pepper for the top of the cone. Fill in with the smaller peppers, arranging the colors to give a balanced composition. Place the peppers together as close as possible. If there are no nails where you want to impale a pepper, take a 5-inch piece of floral wire, bend one end into a hook shape, poke it into the back of the pepper, and slip it under an adjoining pepper, which will anchor the wire in the Spanish moss. This step will help to fill in the open sections of the cone. You can fasten a small pepper to a larger one by impaling the small pepper on a floral wire and pushing the wire into the larger pepper.

Surround the base with broccoli rabe and cayenne peppers, radiating to cover the cardboard.

Use other combinations of vegetables or peppers or place wet floral foam in a bowl and center the cone on the foam to use the cone in different ways. Insert informal summer flowers such as zinnias, solidago, or sage blooms around the base.

After a spicy meal, wedges of watermelon offer a cooling conclusion.

BLACK BEAN, RED PEPPER, AND CORN SALSA

1 jar (16 ounces) medium or hot tomato salsa
juice of 2 limes
1/4 cup red wine vinaigrette

3 cups fresh corn cut from the cob or 1 package (16 ounces) frozen corn, defrosted
2 cans (15 ounces each) black beans, drained and rinsed
1 bunch scallions, finely sliced
1 1/2 cups celery with leaves, finely chopped
1 cup cherry or Italian plum tomatoes cut in half, seeded, chopped, and drained
1 sweet red pepper, minced
3/4 cup cilantro leaves, chopped
1/4 red onion, minced
salt
black pepper, freshly ground
1 jalapeño, seeded and minced (optional)

Mix the salsa, lime juice, and vinaigrette together. Add all remaining ingredients and serve immediately. Increase any of the ingredients to suit your taste. If using the salsa as a salad, reduce the amount of prepared salsa and vinaigrette so it will not be too thin.

A SUMMER GARDEN RECEPTION

Late on a sunny afternoon in the summer, tables set with plantation rum punch and hors d'oeuvres await guests beside the reflecting pool in a walled garden. Flowers bloom in profusion, especially the showy hibiscus. A tablecloth with hand-embroidered hibiscus blossoms blends in perfectly in this semitropical setting.

Plantation rum punch, a favorite summer drink, is served with lime slices and Virginia peanuts.

PLANTATION RUM PUNCH
1 serving

1/2 cup sugar
1/2 cup water
2 ounces rum
dash of bitters
juice of 1/2 lime
crushed ice
nutmeg, freshly grated

Combine the sugar and water in a saucepan and boil for 3 minutes. Cool. In an 8-ounce glass, mix 1 tablespoon of the sugar syrup with the rum, bitters, and lime juice, and fill with crushed ice. Grate fresh nutmeg over the top before serving.

Opposite: Bite-sized slices of seared pork tenderloin and grilled chicken threaded with pineapple chunks accompany the drinks. Fresh fruits look invitingly cool in the heat.

CURRY AND PEANUT DIPPING SAUCE
2 cups

1 cup onion, chopped
2 tablespoons peanut oil
2 medium garlic cloves, minced
3 tablespoons curry powder
2 tablespoons all-purpose flour
2 cups chicken stock, heated
1/4 cup dry white wine or dry vermouth
1 bay leaf
1 teaspoon fresh thyme
3/4 cup whole roasted unsalted peanuts, divided
salt
black pepper, freshly ground

Sauté the onions in the peanut oil over low heat until they are limp and translucent. Stir in the garlic and curry powder and cook for 3 minutes. Blend in the flour, stir to incorporate it, and continue to stir on low heat for another 3 minutes. Add the chicken stock and wine and stir to mix well and to remove any lumps. Add the bay leaf and thyme. Place 1/2 cup of the peanuts in a food processor and grind into a fine meal and add to the mixture. Cook until slightly thickened. Remove the bay leaf. Season with salt and pepper to taste. Place the mixture in the food processor or a blender and puree. If the sauce seems too thick for dipping, it can be thinned with chicken stock. **Note:** Serve with thin slices of grilled pork tenderloin threaded onto bamboo skewers.

Grilled chicken and pork are served with a curry and peanut dipping sauce.

A large bowl of limes and hibiscus blooms adds a colorful touch.

GRILLED CHICKEN AND FRESH PINEAPPLE WITH CHUTNEY
12 servings

6 boneless chicken breasts
1 cup fresh lime juice
olive oil
1 fresh pineapple, cubed
2 cups mango chutney
1 tablespoon kirsch

Marinate the chicken breasts in the lime juice for 2 hours. Brush the breasts with olive oil and grill. Cut the breasts into cubes and thread one piece along with one pineapple chunk on each bamboo skewer. Put the skewers back on the grill long enough to brown the pineapple. Place the mango chutney and kirsch in a food processor and blend until smooth. Serve the chicken with the chutney or the curry and peanut dipping sauce (see page 55).

Macerated fruits and berries, including pineapple, melons, mangoes, green grapes, and peaches, are combined with a splash of lemon juice and kirsch for a rainbow of summer colors that pick up those in the tablecloth, the arrangement of limes and hibiscus, and the potted plants nearby.

OLD FORMS, NEW WAYS: WREATHS

Wreaths made with fresh flowers, fruits, fresh or dried foliage, or berries are among the most adaptable decorations you can create. You can make them in many different sizes using an almost endless variety of plant materials. Try a wreath by itself as a centerpiece or place it around a candlestick and hurricane shade or a decorative object such as a handsome tureen (see page 61). Place one made of pink and white roses, love-in-a-mist, and pink yarrow (see page 60) around the punch bowl at a wedding, or encircle a pumpkin hollowed out to hold soup for a fall luncheon with a ring of autumn leaves. Keep time-honored traditions and use a holly wreath on your front door at Christmas (see page 94) or dare to be different and top your Christmas tree with a wreath of red peppers (see page 118). For other ideas, see pages 60–62, 65, 80, 100, 104–105, 128, 143, 160, and 201.

How to Make a Wreath Using a Floral Foam Form

Supplies and materials needed: Floral foam wreath form with a plastic bottom, floral preservative, clippers, conditioned plant materials (see page 206), and plant mister.

A floral foam wreath form comes in a variety of sizes and, because it retains moisture, allows the use of fresh plant materials over an extended period of time. You should not use it more than once because when the floral foam dries, it will not retain moisture and it could harbor bacteria.

Soak the form in water with floral preservative. Cut 3-inch sprigs of boxwood and remove the bottom inch of leaves from each sprig. Cover the form loosely with the boxwood. Insert the boxwood on an angle that follows the curve of the form.

Insert the flowers and ferns into the form so the colors of the flowers are evenly arranged over the surface and the ferns create graceful accents. The flowers should follow the same direction as the boxwood. Keep the form well watered and mist frequently.

This wreath, as well as many of the following, is placed around a 12-inch-tall hurricane shade, a popular use in Williamsburg.

hurricane shade

fern

fairy rose

mum

Queen Anne's lace

floral foam wreath form

boxwood

Upper left: Yellow and salmon roses are used with intense yellow pixie mums. The base is boxwood. *Upper right:* Blush pink New Dawn and white spray roses and white ranunculus whose edges are tinged with pink are blended with delicate blue love-in-a-mist, purple sea lavender, and pale pink cottage yarrow. They are placed on a seeded eucalyptus wreath. *Lower left:* A variety of herbs including marjoram, rosemary, variegated sage, lemon thyme, pineapple mint, dill, fennel seed heads, basil, lavender, and blossoms of oregano, apple mint, and marjoram are combined with brown-eyed Susans and Montecasino asters on an apple mint base. *Lower right:* Boxwood and rosemary are the base for this wreath of pink fairy roses, bishop's weed, salvia, santolina, and variegated thyme.

Upper left: Oak leaves dipped in glycerin, accented with bittersweet and yarrow, form a ring of autumn colors. *Upper right:* A Christmas wreath of clementines, kumquats, lemons, and red pine cones on floral picks and variegated holly is encircled with Leyland cypress. *Lower left:* A large floral foam wreath used at the base of this imposing goose has been filled with foliage including Leyland cypress, variegated aucuba, variegated holly, and boxwood. *Lower right:* Use a floral foam wreath on top of a larger wreath. Here, a wreath made with pink and white roses *(opposite, upper right)* has been secured to a larger one of dried lavender. The lavender brings out the colors of the love-in-a-mist and the sea lavender.

PRESERVING PLANT MATERIALS

Much has been written on this subject, yet this brief overview will give you the basic information you need to preserve a variety of plant materials. You can dry many flowers, foliage, and herbs so they retain a nearly lifelike appearance, but you need to use the method that works best for the particular plant. You may need to experiment to find the most effective way to retain the color, shape, and, in many cases, fragrance of the plant materials you are preserving. Be warned, however, that some plant materials do not dry well no matter how they are treated. For this reason, cut more plant material than you think you will need.

FLOWERS IN SILICA GEL

Silica gel is easy to use and generally gives good results. It is particularly good for flowers with many petals such as roses. The beauty of this method is that the color, form, and texture of the preserved flower remains remarkably close to the original. Select blooms that are just opening and have firm petals. Pick them on a dry day after the dew has evaporated. The blooms must be completely moisture free before they are put in the silica gel. Flowers that dry well in silica gel include roses, marigolds, feverfew, zinnias, dahlias, peonies, tulips, and daisies.

Dry only one layer of flowers at a time. Flowers with flat blooms, such as daisies or marigolds, should be dried face down. Dry flowers such as roses or bell-shaped flowers face up.

Select a container with a lid that will hold the flowers you are preserving. You can use various types and sizes of containers, from cardboard boxes to cookie tins. Silica gel must be completely dry before it is used and should be kept in an airtight, covered container. After using it, dry the silica gel in the oven to restore its original color. It is important to always wear a mask when using silica gel.

When drying a rose or any bell-shaped flower, put 1 inch of silica gel over the bottom of the container. Remove all but 1 inch of the stem from the flower and insert a 3-inch piece of #28 gauge floral wire from the base of the stem through the center of the flower. Bend the end of the floral wire to form a slight hook and pull it back so the hook is hidden in the center of the flower. Bend the floral wire carefully at right angles to the base of the flower. Nestle the bloom into the silica gel in the container. Use a spoon to put a collar of silica gel around the outside of the bloom to support the petals, then gently sift some silica gel over the center of the flower. This procedure allows the flower to retain its original shape. Cover the flower to a depth of about $1/2$ inch with silica gel and tightly cover the container.

Dry like flowers together so the drying time will be consistent for that particular container. Label the container with the contents and date to help you keep track of the time needed to thoroughly dry each batch of flowers. Experimentation will help you determine the amount of time it will take. Small flowers will only take 1 or 2 days to dry. Some fleshy flowers will take longer. Roses, for instance, will take between 4 and 7 days to dry. When you check to see whether the materials are dry, open the container and, wearing a mask, gently shake it to uncover the flowers. Remove one bloom with a slotted spoon. If it appears to be totally dry, gently pour the crystals back into the container. Remove flowers one at a time, straighten the floral wire, and insert it in a block of floral foam to protect the flower from rubbing against other blooms.

If any silica gel clings to the petals, remove it with a soft paintbrush. If a petal should fall off, re-attach it by putting a dab of white glue on the base of the petal and another where the petals overlap to hold the fallen petal in place. The stems of most flowers you dry will be too short to use in an arrangement. Make a longer stem by inserting the short stem of your flower into a dried stem of cockscomb, yarrow, delphinium, or other long, dried stems, including those of grasses or grains. If the stem of your flower is too wide to fit into a long, dried stem, connect the two with a 3-inch piece of #18 gauge floral wire.

Opposite: The close up *(above)* shows dried orange slices and Chinese lanterns combined with fresh materials in a foam wreath. Always attach dried materials to wet floral foam by securing them on wooden picks or wire, and then insert them into the foam. The Chinese lanterns on this wreath *(left)* have been cut to form star-shaped flowers.

All drying techniques were used is these arrangements *(above* and *opposite)*. Most of the plant materials have been preserved in silica gel, by air drying, or in glycerin.

FOLIAGE IN GLYCERIN

Preserve a variety of tree or shrub leaves with a glycerin solution. Many will turn a beautiful bronze, russet, or almost black color and become pliable, glossy, and long lasting as the solution is absorbed. This technique is particularly successful when used with foliage from magnolias and other broad-leafed trees such as bay, camellia, and beach. Experiment with other leaves including laurel, oak, and Russian olive.

You can purchase glycerin at pharmacies, in some craft stores, and from floral supply firms. To prepare the mixture, mix one part glycerin with three parts hot water. Mix thoroughly until the solution is clear. Put 3 inches of the mixture into a glass jar so the liquid will be well above the cut ends of the stems.

Use only mature foliage. Prune each branch into the size and shape you plan to use for your arrangement. Check for imperfections and remove any leaves with insect damage. Clean the foliage in warm water. It is important to have the hot glycerin mixture ready before cutting the end. Cut the base of the stem on the diagonal, then make 1-inch vertical slits at the base, which will help with absorption of the solution.

To prevent the weight of the branches from tipping over the jar, put the jar into a pail and wedge it against one side of the pail with a brick or a stone. Watch the liquid level carefully during this period, replenishing when necessary as it is absorbed. Remove the foliage from the liquid when the top leaves become brown and glossy, usually in about 1 to 3 weeks.

To preserve individual leaves, put them in a shallow dish and cover the leaves with the solution. They will change quickly. You can also treat ivy strands in this way. If foliage becomes dull looking after being preserved and used, gently dust and rub the leaves with mineral oil to return their shine.

Oak leaves treated with glycerin become a rich reddish bronze. Here they are tucked into a grapevine wreath with bittersweet.

AIR DRYING PLANT MATERIALS

Many flowers can be hung upside down and dried in small bunches. Others, such as Queen Anne's lace, do well when placed right side up on a drying tray with a clothespin holding the stem close to the wire mesh to keep the bloom from leaning. Other plant materials, many with interesting seed heads, pods, or cones, often dry naturally in the field.

Because many plant materials will dry bent if dried upright, remove the lower leaves and secure the flowers or foliage in small bunches with a rubber band. Hang the bunches upside down over a taut clothesline in a warm, dry, dark location near a heat source, in a dry attic, or along the sides of a drying rack. Do not crowd the bunches. Flowers and foliage that do well drying by this method include heather, pussy willow, globe amaranth, globe thistle, goldenrod, yar-row, tansy, salvia, cockscomb, lavender, baby's breath, strawflower, statice, mountain mint, love-in-a-mist, artemisia, and dock.

Most fresh herbs used in a wreath or a "faux" topiary will dry as the floral foam dries. To make these decorations, start with a wet floral foam wreath form, or a wet block of floral foam on a topiary base. Make the wreath or topiary following the directions on pages 58 and 70. Insert the plant materials at angles facing the same direction to achieve the best coverage. Because the drying process will shrink the plant materials, you will need to pack them tightly into the form. As the herbs dry, most remain fragrant and will cover the form because they are tightly packed. After the wreath or topiary has dried, add strawflowers and other colorful dried blooms for accent or to fill in a hole. When starting with dried materials, use a dry floral foam form.

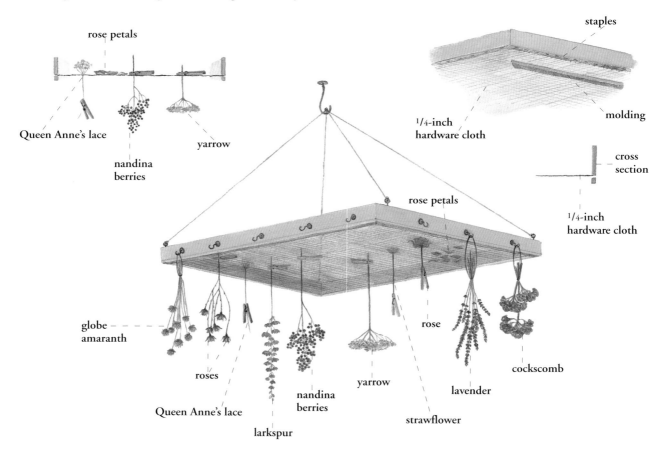

PRESSING PLANT MATERIALS

Use a plant press to press flowers and foliage for framing or to use in decoupage or in other crafts. Show one type of flower or plant, such as a fern, in different stages of development. Use acid-free newsprint and blotting paper, which are available in craft stores or from archival supply sources.

How to Make a Plant Press

Supplies and materials needed: Clamps, two pieces of 10 x 12 x 1/2 inch plywood board, drill with 5/16-inch bit, four 1/4-inch screws 4 inches long with matching washers and wing nuts, acid-free blotting paper, and acid-free newsprint.

Clamp the two boards together, one on top of the other, and drill four 5/16-inch holes through both boards 3/4-inch in from each corner. Place washers on the screws and slip them through the holes.

Cut five pieces of acid-free blotting paper to fit on the bottom board and put the sheets on the board. Cut the corners at an angle to fit around the screws. Cut two pieces of acid-free newsprint the same size with the corners angled and put them on top of the blotting paper.

Carefully arrange the plant materials on the newsprint sheets. In placing the specimens, consider how they will be used: framed, glued on a note card, applied as a decoration for decoupage, or for other projects.

Cover the plant materials with two sheets of newsprint, then two sheets of blotting paper. Repeat this layering process until you have placed all the materials you wish to dry in the press. Cover the top layer with the top board and tighten the wing nuts gradually until all four corners are secure.

Leave the materials for 7 days before you open the press. Open it carefully in case your materials are not completely dry and need to be pressed for a few more days. **Note:** Use 3/4-inch-thick plywood for a larger press.

DRYING FRUIT AND NUTS

Use a dehydrator with its gauge set for the correct temperature for the kind of fruit you select or an oven with a setting of 150°F. or lower to produce beautiful dried fruit slices. Citrus fruit, apples that have been dipped in lemon juice, apricots, or guava can be used for garlands or as accents in decorations. Check the fruit periodically to see whether it is dry. You can also dry nuts in a dehydrator or in an oven. The heat will kill any dormant insects. Dry nuts the same length of time as fruit. Collect pods, nuts, cones, and other interesting dried materials throughout the year and store them with insect preventative in dust-proof containers. You will soon have plenty of materials on hand for making a wreath for your door, a garland for your mantel, or perhaps a dried cone for your table.

STORAGE OF PRESERVED MATERIALS

An airtight container and a dry storage area are keys to extending the life of dried flowers and foliage. A dehumidifier used in the storage area is helpful if you hang plant materials to dry. Dried flowers and foliage store well in dry floral foam or in sealed tins in which a small amount of silica gel has been added. It is most important that you not crowd the flowers and foliage. Many floral sprays are available to add stability to blooms. If you use one of these sprays, apply it lightly on the face and heavily on the back when the flower has first been dried.

Dried fruit can be stored in airtight containers much the same as flowers with a bit of silica gel under a layer of tissue paper. Often citrus slices will turn black after an extended period, but whole dried oranges will last indefinitely if kept dry. Nuts and raisin chains can be stored in the freezer in a freezer bag.

INDIAN SUMMER LUNCHEON

Noon on the marsh is a tranquil time. Sunlight filters through the oak trees, great blue herons fish the still waters, and monarch butterflies silently flutter to nearby flowers.

The table setting mirrors the woodsy surroundings. A large knot cut from a tree holds a small fern. Ferns are repeated on the tablecloth and stamped on the napkins. Bronze frogs peek from under ferns, grasses, pieris, and weeds that fill the candlesticks. Wild mushroom soup, its surface circled with cream, is served in wooden bowls on chargers. A trug is filled with a rustic herb cheese bread.

WILD MUSHROOM SOUP
6 servings

1 large, sweet onion, roughly chopped

2 large shallots, roughly chopped

4 tablespoons unsalted butter

2 tablespoons olive oil

2 pounds mushrooms, any combination of
    domestic and wild, divided

2 tablespoons lemon juice

4 cups unsalted chicken stock

1/4 cup dry sherry

1 tablespoon mushroom base
    concentrate (optional)

2 teaspoons dried thyme or 1 heaping
    tablespoon fresh thyme (or more to taste)

1 tablespoon minced parsley plus 6 sprigs

salt and pepper

2 cups half-and-half, divided

1 tablespoon minced fresh chives

nutmeg, freshly grated

Sauté the onions and shallots in the butter and olive oil until transparent. Trim and discard the stems from the mushrooms. Set aside six. Roughly chop the rest and add them to the onions and shallots. Sauté for 5 minutes while stirring over medium heat. Add the lemon juice and let the mushroom mixture cool. Heat the chicken stock, sherry, mushroom base, thyme, and parsley in a separate pan and bring to a boil. Reduce the heat and simmer for 5 minutes. Place the mushroom mixture in a food processor and puree until almost smooth. If it is too thick, add some of the seasoned chicken stock. Add salt and pepper to taste. Add the mushroom mixture to the seasoned chicken stock and bring to a simmer. To serve, sauté the remaining mushrooms. Add 1 1/2 cups of the cream and bring the soup back to a simmer. Do not let the soup come to a boil. Put the remaining cream into a soft plastic bottle with a nozzle. Before serving, swirl a circle of cream on the surface of each serving. Garnish with parsley, chives, a mushroom, and nutmeg.

OLD FORMS, NEW WAYS
"FAUX" TOPIARIES

These decorative trees can be almost any size, from over six feet to under twelve inches, made with fresh or dried materials, and embellished with garden or field flowers, fruit, herbs, berries, pods, cones, ferns, and foliage. See pages 71–73, 138, and 170 for other "faux" topiaries.

Upper row, left to right: Roses and iris are interspersed with solidago and variegated pittosporum on the form. Small iris, roses, bouvardia, and Alexandrian laurel are combined here. Lisianthus, roses, lilacs, and Queen Anne's lace are accented with variegated pittosporum and Alexandrian laurel. *Lower row, left to right:* Roses, salvia, candytuft, and leptospermum are used with tiny forget-me-nots at the base. Daisies, Queen Anne's lace, delphinium, and solidago dominate this late summer topiary. Siberian iris, anemones, and bouvardia make a bold statement. *Opposite:* Christmas brings a partridge in a pear tree *(above)* to the St. George Tucker House. The lemon topiary *(left)* is ready to be used inside or on a deck or terrace.

71

How to Make a Reusuable "Faux" Topiary Using Fresh Flowers and Fruit

Supplies and materials needed: Branch, decorative container, plastic liner, masking tape, plaster of paris, paint stirrer, instant deluxe floral foam, floral preservative, conditioned plant materials (see page 206), fruit (optional), wooden picks, #22 gauge green floral wire, sheet or Spanish moss, funnel, and plant mister.

Cut a branch and make a point at one end. An unusual one with moss growing on it, or whose bark varies in color, is a good choice. The height of the branch is determined by the height of your decoration. Decide on the height of the finished piece then subtract approximately 5 inches to give you the height of the branch. As a rule, the branch will be roughly three times the height of the container. A tall topiary requires a heavy branch and a larger floral foam block that should be covered with deer netting or other lightweight netting.

Select a decorative container suitable for the size of topiary you are making and a plastic liner that will fit inside it. Tape over any drainage holes in the liner with masking tape. Fill the liner almost to the top with plaster of paris. Add water and stir quickly. Add more water or plaster of paris as needed and thoroughly mix the ingredients until the plaster of paris is smooth and thick. Insert the blunt end of the branch, checking that it is centered and vertical. Let the plaster of paris dry for 24 hours, then place the liner into the outside container. Using a removeable liner for the form will free the decorative outside container for other uses.

The size of the floral block depends on the size of topiary you are making. A 20-inch-tall topiary will require half a block. Trim off the corners and soak in

Chinese lanterns, dried orange slices, and the berries of Alexandrian laurel foliage, all of whose colors suggest fall, are combined with white spray roses and white asters.

water with floral preservative. Push the foam down onto the stick. Omit soaking the foam when using only dried materials or fruits.

Boxwood is often used as a base, but other well-conditioned materials can be substituted, such as ivy, aucuba, pittosporum, Alexandrian laurel, or pieris. Green or variegated foliage adds interest. Cut the stems on the diagonal into 4- to 5-inch pieces, and strip any leaves from the bottom 1 1/2 inches of the stems. Keep the stems in water as you work. Insert stems into the foam until the foam is loosely covered. This light covering will allow room for flowers. Cut the stems of the flowers on an angle and insert them into the foam, making sure that no two flowers are too close, that they do not form a line in any direction, and that they face in different directions. Floral materials that differ in textures and sizes make interesting combinations. Colors can be monochromatic or varied. As you insert the flowers, keep turning the container to distribute them evenly. If using fruits, impale them on wooden picks and insert them in the floral foam. These picks come in many sizes. A 6-inch pick was used for the lemons on the lemon topiary; a 4-inch pick, for the Chinese lanterns. When using a dehydrated fruit slice, cut a 6-inch piece of floral wire, poke it through the fruit near the rind, twist the wire around itself, and insert it into the foam.

Cover the top of the container with dampened green sheet moss or Spanish moss. Add clumps of small plants tucked in the moss, such as Johnny-jump-ups or forget-me-nots for a springtime topiary, and berries or acorns in season.

To water, cover the top of the container with a dish towel, then insert a funnel into the top of the foam. Water slowly until it starts to drip. When the water stops dripping, remove the towel.

Place the topiary away from direct heat and bright light and keep it well watered and misted. **Note:** This "faux" topiary form can be reused many times if you replace the floral foam.

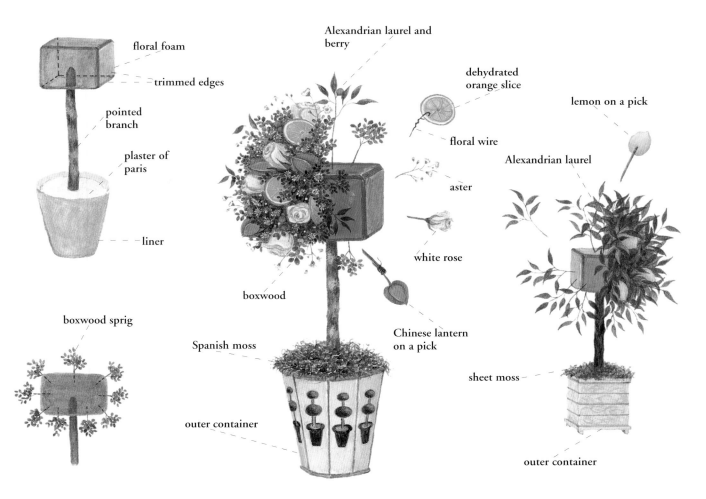

floral foam

trimmed edges

pointed branch

plaster of paris

liner

boxwood sprig

Alexandrian laurel and berry

dehydrated orange slice

floral wire

aster

white rose

boxwood

Spanish moss

outer container

Chinese lantern on a pick

lemon on a pick

Alexandrian laurel

sheet moss

outer container

A basket of crisp applesauce tarts seasoned with rosemary, the herb of remembrance, sits atop a barrel made by Colonial Williamsburg's cooper in the orchard beside the Lightfoot House.

AUTUMN APPLES

One of the joys of fall is to cook with the many different kinds of apples available at roadside stands and farmers' markets. Apples were abundant in eighteenth-century Virginia orchards. One of Thomas Jefferson's favorite varieties, called 'Esopus Spitzenburg,' is still available and planted in Williamsburg's gardens.

ROSEMARY APPLESAUCE TARTS
8 to 10 tarts

1/3 cup plus 1/2 cup apricot preserves, divided
5 tablespoons apple brandy, divided
1 tablespoon rosemary
8 cups apples
2/3 cup plus 2 tablespoons sugar, divided
3 tablespoons unsalted butter
1/2 teaspoon cinnamon
1 tablespoon orange zest
1/2 teaspoon rosemary, finely chopped
1/2 cup walnuts, finely chopped
1 1/2 cups all-purpose flour
1/2 cup butter, cut into pieces
1/4 cup ice water

Heat 1/3 cup apricot preserves, 4 tablespoons brandy, and rosemary. Cool and steep overnight. Quarter, core, and peel the apples, cut them in rough slices, and cook covered, over low heat, for 20 minutes, stirring occasionally, until tender. Reheat the apricot preserve mixture, then strain. Combine the apples with the apricot preserve mixture, 2/3 cup sugar, unsalted butter, cinnamon, and zest. Bring to a boil, stirring until applesauce is thick enough to hold in a mass on a spoon. To prepare the pastry, preheat the oven to 375°F. Lightly oil eight to ten 4-inch tart pans. Place the finely chopped rosemary, walnuts, and flour in a food processor and combine. Add the pieces of butter and process until the mixture has the texture of cornmeal. Add the ice water and process until the dough is formed into a ball. Roll out the dough, line the prepared tart pans with the pastry, and fill with applesauce. Top each tart with thin lattice strips cut from the pastry. Bake at 375°F. for 15 minutes or until golden. While the tarts are baking, make the glaze by stirring 1/2 cup apricot preserves and 2 tablespoons sugar over medium-high heat for 2 to 3 minutes. Add the remaining brandy and strain. Immediately after removing the tarts from the oven, brush them with the glaze.

APPLE AND PEANUT GRANOLA FROM THE WILLIAMSBURG INN

4 cups rolled oats
1 cup whole bran cereal
1 cup whole wheat flour
1 cup coconut, grated
1 cup peanuts
1/2 cup light brown sugar, packed
1/2 cup butter
1/2 cup honey
2 teaspoons cinnamon
1 teaspoon nutmeg
1/4 teaspoon salt
2 teaspoons vanilla
1/4 cup raisins or currants
1 cup slivered almonds, toasted
1 Granny Smith apple, cored and chopped

Preheat the oven to 275°F. Mix oats, bran, flour, coconut, and peanuts in a large roasting pan. Combine the sugar, butter, honey, cinnamon, nutmeg, and salt in a small pan and bring to a boil. Remove from the heat and add the vanilla. Pour over the dry ingredients and mix well. Bake at 275°F. for 1 hour for a soft granola, or for 2 hours for a crunchy granola. Stir the cereal every 15 minutes. Remove from the oven and add the raisins or currants and almonds. Cool and put into an airtight container. Add the chopped Granny Smith apple before serving. **Note:** You can add additional nuts or fruits.

HALLOWEEN

This is the time of year when you can combine the rich array of plant materials from your fall garden to create a vibrant wreath, decorations, and food for a harvest brunch, or to decorate a door to welcome young goblins who will come trick-or-treating.

Here a colorful wreath hangs on the door and a friendly serpent, a pumpkin snowman with shredded corn-husk hair and twig arms, and other gourd creatures await the arrival of young ghosts, pirates, and witches.

To make the pumpkin snowman, you will need three pumpkins of decreasing size. Carve a face in the smallest pumpkin. Remove the stems from the two larger ones and stack the three. Select two twig branches for arms, cut holes for them in the middle pumpkin, then insert one branch in each hole. To shred cornhusks for his hair, hold a husk by its narrow end and pierce the husk with a pin 1/2 inch from the end. Pull the pin through to the other end and repeat until the section is shredded.

To make the gourd serpent, select a twisted gourd and then impale an apricot and a raisin on a round-headed pin for each eye and push the pins into the gourd. Carve a slit for the mouth and insert a fresh pineapple sage blossom for its tongue.

A Halloween party for children is always fun. An orange-and-black checked cloth is covered with Halloween treats. A ring of paper bats glued to short skewers guards the cider punch, and bowls of icings, paintbrushes, and sugar cookies (see page 152) are set out for the Halloween artists. Small pumpkins wear the many faces of Halloween and a gourd basket is filled with candy corn.

How to Make Halloween Crackers

In England, Christmas crackers are a tradition on holiday tables; here, having children make them for Halloween adds to the festivities. Assemble the supplies and have plenty of paper patterns, stamps, ink pads, and pictures for decorating. Paper punches are fun to use to make Halloween shapes.

Supplies and materials needed: Scissors, ruler, orange and/or black tissue or crepe paper, 5 x 1 1/2 inch cardboard tubes from rolls of kitchen towels or waxed paper, party hats, jokes, fortunes, tiny presents, double-sided tape, ribbon, stickers, glue, paper cutouts, and/or stamps and ink pads.

Cut one 12 x 6 1/2 inch piece of the paper or two different colored pieces. If you use two colors, cut the second one 1 inch shorter in length. If using tissue paper, you will need two thicknesses to cover each tube.

Center the tube near the edge of one of the long sides, leaving equal lengths of paper on each end. Before covering the tube, tuck party favors (such as a party hat, joke, fortune, or other tiny presents) inside. Roll the paper tightly over the tube and secure it with double-sided tape. Tie each end with ribbon. Decorate each tube with stickers, cutouts, and/or stamped designs.

How to Make a Cornhusk Wreath

Supplies and materials needed: Straw wreath form, tan chenille wire, cornhusks, floral pins, minipumpkins, gourds, #18 gauge green floral wire, wire cutters, seeded eucalyptus, yarrow, fall leaves, and 3-inch wired wooden floral picks.

This wreath can be made with a variety of plant materials and colors. Use a ready-made cornhusk wreath and add the materials as suggested or follow the directions to make one yourself.

Select a straw wreath form. Take a chenille wire and loop it around the wreath, twist it in back, and form a loop for the hanger. Using dried corn-husks (available in craft stores), separate the husks and spray or soak them in water to soften. Fold each husk in half, one at a time, to form a loop and then gather the ends together. Secure the ends to the straw form with floral pins. Continue around the form in one direc-tion, pinning the loops along the outside and inside edges as well as on the top as shown. Slightly vary the angles of the loops to give a softer look. Continue around the wreath until the entire form is covered with loops. The ends of the loops on the last row should be pinned under the loops of the first row.

To decorate the wreath, start your design with the most dominant plant material. It is helpful to place the wreath on a flat surface and try different arrangements of the materials before securing them to the form. In this example, the minipumpkins and gourds are arranged in a symmetrical pattern. Pierce each pumpkin or gourd horizontally with floral wire. Bend the wire down and wrap it around the wreath form, twisting the two wire ends together on the inside of the wreath to secure them. Trim off the long ends and

conceal the cut ends under the loops to prevent scratching the door or wall on which you hang the wreath or the surface of a table on which you might place it.

Tightly wrap small bunches of the seeded eucalyptus, yarrow, cornhusks you have shredded, and leaves using floral picks, making each bunch about 4 inches long. Tuck them between the gourds and pumpkins, and push the floral pick into the straw form to secure the bunches. Be careful to conceal the mechanics under the loops. **Note:** Select gourds without varnish or blemishes, remove the dirt, and soak for 5 minutes in a solution of one part bleach to two parts water to eliminate bacteria. Let them dry.

shredded cornhusk

chenille wire loop

seeded eucalyptus
on floral pick

floral pick

straw wreath

cornhusk loop

start here

oak leaf on
floral pick

floral pin

wired minipumpkin

gourd

yarrow

floral wire

HARVEST BRUNCH

The table is set for a bountiful harvest brunch with a carved wooden chicken and rooster standing among corn kernels, miniature ears of Indian corn, spatter-painted eggs in Staffordshire eggcups, and wheat tied with raffia in pottery candlesticks, all adding to the color and feel of fall. The fragrance of sliced zucchini, summer squash, and fresh tomatoes on a bed of caramelized onions and fresh thyme fills the room.

ized onions and garlic over the bottom, and sprinkle generously with about 1 tablespoon fresh thyme. Slice the tomatoes and drain on a paper towel. Slice the summer squash and zucchini at a slight angle, approximately 1/4-inch thick, and toss with the remaining olive oil and remaining fresh thyme. Lean a row of upright tomato slices across the width of the dish over the onions and sprinkle cheese on the cut surfaces. Partially overlap the row of tomatoes with a row of yellow squash and a row of zucchini both interspersed with cheese. Continue alternating the sliced vegetables and cheese until the dish is filled. Add salt and pepper, sprinkle the remaining cheese, and drizzle the olive oil and thyme over the top. Bake at 350°F. for 45 minutes to 1 hour or until the cheese is melted and the casserole is lightly browned. Serve hot. **Note:** When selecting the summer squash and zucchini, choose squash of equal diameter to the tomatoes if possible.

FALL VEGETABLE CASSEROLE
8 servings

2 large, sweet onions
2 tablespoons olive oil, divided
1 large clove garlic, minced
coarse salt
2 tablespoons fresh thyme, divided
1 pound Italian plum tomatoes
3/4 pound summer squash, small and firm
3/4 pound zucchini
11/4 cups Parmesan cheese, grated and divided
pepper

Preheat the oven to 350°F. Cut the onions in quarters and slice very thinly. Cook them over medium heat with 1 tablespoon olive oil or enough to coat the bottom of the pan. Cover, and leave them until they start to caramelize, approximately 30 to 45 minutes. After the onions begin to caramelize, stir frequently for about 5 minutes until they are golden brown. Add the garlic, stir well, and remove the onions from the heat. Lightly salt the onions and set aside to cool. Oil a 2-quart shallow baking dish, spread the caramel-

Scrambled eggs with diced sweet red peppers stay warm in a chafing dish and are accompanied by piping hot corn bread sticks.

GAME PÂTÉ

3/4 pound bacon strips

1 tablespoon butter

1 medium onion, finely chopped

4 garlic cloves, minced

2 large eggs, well beaten

1/2 cup brandy

2 tablespoons fresh rosemary, minced

1 teaspoon ground coriander

1 tablespoon fresh thyme, minced

1/8 teaspoon nutmeg

1/8 teaspoon cloves

2 teaspoons plus 1 pinch salt

2 teaspoons pepper, freshly ground

1 1/2 pounds pheasant or other game fowl, ground,
   or ground turkey

3/4 pound pork sausage

1/2 pound Virginia ham, unsliced

2 egg whites

6 bay leaves

Preheat the oven to 450°F. Lay the bacon strips on a nonstick baking sheet and bake them for 5 minutes, drain off the fat, and set the strips aside. Lower the oven to 350°F. Melt the butter in a medium skillet. Add the onions and sauté over medium heat until translucent but not brown. Add the garlic and cook for 2 more minutes then set aside. Combine the eggs with the brandy, rosemary, coriander, thyme, nutmeg, cloves, 2 teaspoons salt, and pepper, mixing well until blended. Combine the pheasant or other fowl and the sausage with the onions and garlic in an electric mixer, add the brandy mixture, and mix together just long enough to incorporate the ingredients evenly. Cover and refrigerate for several hours. Slice the Virginia ham into thin strips. Beat the egg whites with a pinch of salt until stiff. Set aside 2 tablespoons and fold the remaining whites into the spinach-mushroom filling. Line a 1 1/2-quart terrine with the bacon. Arrange the strips so there will be enough overhang to cover the pâté after the terrine is filled. Spread a 1 1/2-inch layer of the pâté mixture in the bottom of the terrine. Press down with a spatula. Arrange a layer lengthwise of the ham strips on top of the pâté mixture. Using a pastry brush, coat the ham with some of the beaten egg whites to bind the vegetables and meat. Cover with a layer of the spinach-mushroom filling, pack it down, and spread with a layer of egg white. Add a second layer of the pâté mixture, ham strips, egg white, and spinach-mushroom filling, packed down, and top with egg white. Finish with a third layer of pâté mixture, pack it down, and smooth the surface. Fold the bacon over the top. Place the bay leaves on top of the bacon. Cover with a double thickness of aluminum foil. Put the lid on the terrine and place the terrine in a roasting pan. Fill the pan with enough hot water to come two-thirds of the way up the sides of the terrine and bake at 350°F. for 1 hour 15 minutes. Remove the terrine from the water bath. Take off the lid and put a heavy object such as a brick wrapped in foil on top of the pâté to weigh it down. Cool completely. Refrigerate, covered, for at least 2 days. **Note:** The meats for the pâté should be finely ground. When using whole game fowl, cut the meat from the bones, remove the tendons, and cut it into cubes. Freeze the meat for 40 minutes before grinding. Save any remaining spinach-mushroom filling to add to your next family meat loaf or to a bowl of soup.

SPINACH-MUSHROOM FILLING

1 box (10 ounces) frozen chopped spinach
1 medium onion, finely chopped
2 tablespoons butter
1 pound shitake or other mushrooms, stems
    removed
1 tablespoon lemon juice
1/2 teaspoon salt
1/4 teaspoon pepper, freshly ground
1/4 cup brandy
1/2 cup whipping cream
2 pinches nutmeg
1 pinch cloves
3/4 teaspoon fresh rosemary, minced
1/3 cup parsley, chopped
1 cup walnuts, chopped

Defrost the spinach and drain it, wringing out excess moisture in a towel. Sauté the onions in the butter until translucent. Place the mushrooms in a food processor and chop. Add the mushrooms to the onions and sauté until the juices are reduced. Add the lemon juice, salt, pepper, and brandy, and continue to cook until the liquid is reduced. Add the cream and cook until it is reduced. Add the spinach, nutmeg, cloves, rosemary, and parsley to the mushroom mixture, blending well. Mix in the walnuts.

Country ham is surrounded with grapes, spiced apple rings, and pickled peaches. Hollowed out gourds and turban squash are filled with pepper and corn relishes.

85

ONE SETTING, FIVE IDEAS

The Coke-Garrett House dining room is noted for its striking scenic wall paper, *Les Vues de l'Amérique du Nord,* a modern block-printed rendition of the 1834–1836 pattern designed by Jean-Julien Deltil. The somewhat fanciful scenes that encircle the room are based on early nineteenth-century engravings, the period in which this section of the house was built. Virginia's Natural Bridge, West Point, Boston Harbor, and Niagara Falls are among the scenes depicted.

Here two arrangements of fall plant materials and one of spring flowers, using colors to harmonize with the wallpaper, create different effects on the dining room table. *Above:* Blocks of floral foam covered with galax leaves, bittersweet, and fall leaves accentuate the rich rusts and golds in the paper. Acorns, assorted nuts, gourds, and minipumpkins surround the base. *Left:* Two silver beakers filled with red and pink roses and chrysanthemums are softened by the pale tan of the autumn fern foliage, the same color as the sails and packing boxes on the dock seen in the wallpaper.

Opposite: This arrangement brings a burst of glorious color to the table. Violas, pansies, roses, ranunculus, anemones, and other blooms on the antique English dessert service from about 1820 inspired the choice of flowers for the centerpiece.

Colors in this arrangement of brilliant yellow poplar leaves, nandina berries in varying stages of ripeness, rose hips, and pyracantha berries enhance those of the imposing figure on the left and of the elegantly dressed ladies and gentlemen on horseback on the right.

A different look in the same location is achieved by using red oak leaves, dark green foliage, and pineapple sage foliage and blooms. Ripening nandina and hypericum berries spill over the sides of the urn.

CONTAINER GARDENS

The chill of late fall makes you think about the coming winter and how you can brighten and fill your house with wonderful fragrance and colorful flowers during the darkest days of the year. Try bringing out bulbs you planted in pots in the fall and watching them burst into bloom or create a dish garden, always popular to use in the home. Properly maintained, they will flourish for a long time. Dish gardens, along with bulb gardens, warm the heart of any gardener in winter.

How to Plant Bulbs in Pots for Forcing

Supplies and materials needed: Spring-flowering bulbs, pot, nylon window screening, potting soil, and sheet or Spanish moss.

Some of the most successful bulbs for forcing are the fragrant hyacinths, crocuses, miniature daffodils, paper-white narcissus, amaryllis, and grape hyacinths. When planting more than one variety of bulb in the same container, select ones that will blossom at the same time. Or you may wish to layer several kinds of bulbs in a larger container to produce intermittent blooming.

To trick plants into thinking that winter is over and it is time to flower, plant the bulbs, except for paper-white narcissus and amaryllis, about 3 months before you want them to bloom. Bulbs purchased in the summer should be stored in a cool, dry place until you plant them in the fall.

Select firm and compact bulbs, never ones that are soft or sprouting. Use a clean pot and cover drainage holes with pieces of screening. Fill all but the top 2 inches of the pot with potting soil. To make the best show when blooming, position as many bulbs as will fit into a pot with their tips upward and the bulbs almost touching. Do not let them touch the sides of the pot; the tips should be just below the rim of the

This clay pot is planted with a colorful assortment of bleeding hearts dug from a spring garden, miniature daffodils, tulips, and Johnny-jump-ups planted in the fall.

pot. Cover them with the soil, firming it around the bulbs so the tops are just visible. Water the bulbs well to settle the potting soil and then add moss. Keep the soil slightly moist but never wet. Bulbs do well in potting soil with good drainage. Keep the bulbs in a cool, dry place such as an old refrigerator without dehumidification control, a root cellar, or a basement. During this period, the bulbs will grow a strong root system. Bulbs should be left in a cool area for at least 3 months (see the Bulb Forcing Timetable on page 92). During this time, you will see shoots coming up and roots coming up out of the soil or the gravel.

Be sure to label and date the pot so you will know when to bring it out of storage. Once the bulbs

Opposite: A fragrant container garden *(above)* created with rosemary topiaries, paper-white narcissus, pink and white cyclamen, and ivy is displayed on a window seat in the Lightfoot House. The wreath is made in two parts. The outer ring of roses has been placed on a base of noble fir.

have had time to establish strong root systems, they can be brought gradually into the warmth of the house. Light and warmth will promote the growth of the leaves and flowers. Start by putting them into an area with indirect sunlight and a 50°F. temperature for about a week. Once the shoots are 4 to 6 inches high, they can be placed into bright sunlight and in a temperature of about 68°F. When the bulbs start to bloom, put them back into indirect sunlight so the flowers will last longer. During this period, the soil should be kept moist but not wet.

Paper-white narcissus bulbs may be grown in soil or gravel in a shallow bowl following the same directions or planted in the bottom of a tall glass container whose sides will support their leaves. If you use a glass container, put only a small amount of gravel, not soil, at the bottom.

Amaryllis bulbs need to be planted near the top of the container. Although they can be planted and put in the house immediately, paper-white narcissus and amaryllis bulbs will benefit from being kept in a lower temperature after potting, 45 to 50°F. for about 2 weeks, and in low light. After this period, when the roots have formed a strong system, they can be moved into the sunlight. At this point, you can expect them to bloom in another week or two. If paper-white narcissus and amaryllis are planted according to the timetable, you can look forward to an early spring in December. **Note:** If you want flowers throughout the season, stagger the plantings in multiple containers.

Bulb Forcing Timetable

BULB NAME	WEEKS OF COLD	WEEKS TO BLOOM
Amaryllis	none	6 to 8
Dwarf iris	15	2 to 3
Dutch crocus	15	2
Frittilaria	15	3
Glory-of-the-snow	15	2 to 3
Grape hyacinth	13 to 15	2 to 3
Hyacinth	11 to 14	2 to 3
Miniature daffodil	12 to 14	2 to 3
Paper-white narcissus	none	3 to 5
Scilla	15	2 to 3
Snowdrop	15	2
Tulip	14 to 20	2 to 3
Winter aconite	15	2

How to Plant a Dish Garden

A small ebony spleenwort is planted in a container, then mosses, lichens, acorns, and partridgeberry plants are added.

Supplies and materials needed: A variety of plant materials, a low container, nylon window screening or gravel, charcoal, potting soil, and sheet or Spanish moss (optional).

Select plants that require the same amount of light, moisture, and temperature range, and are compatible in size with the container you are using. Plants should have a variety of color and texture and can be all blooming, all nonblooming, or a combination of both. Potted blooming plants can be added. All potted plants should be turned occasionally. If you use a flowering potted plant, you can remove it and replace it with another plant after it finishes blooming.

Find a container that has enough room and proper drainage for the plants you have chosen. Place a piece of nylon screening over the drainage holes. If you are using a container without drainage holes, put 1 or 2 inches of gravel in the bottom to supply drainage, and add a thin layer of charcoal, such as the type available at a tropical fish store. Place soil on top of the screening or gravel and charcoal layers, if used, and then add plant materials such as potted miniature roses, begonias, and ivy used here. Once the garden is planted, cover the surface with moss. If you use plants with thick foliage, this covering will not be necessary. You can fill your container with plants dug from your garden or potted materials from a nursery.

potted miniature rose

begonia

ivy

gravel

A vibrant holly wreath on the beautifully false-grained front door of the Coke-Garrett House signals the start of Christmas in Williamsburg. Each sprig of holly is attached to a pick and then inserted into a straw wreath base.

CHRISTMAS IN WILLIAMSBURG

Colonial Williamsburg has long been noted for its Christmas decorations using natural plant materials, many from its gardens. Immediately after Thanksgiving is a good time to inventory your garden and canvas your local nursery for fruits and greens, pods and berries, or nuts and cones that you can turn into wreaths, table, mantel, or wall arrangements, or ornaments for a special Christmas tree. Consider bringing living materials inside, such as tabletop trees, then planting them after Christmas. They can be kept inside for a week. Take fruits and seeds outside to decorate a tree in your garden that will attract many different kinds of birds during and after the holidays.

CHRISTMAS DECORATIONS

A pair of dwarf Alberta spruce trees in lightly gilded pots helps to coordinate the colorful mantel decorations and garlands with the table settings. The tiny living tabletop trees are decorated with gold cording and berries of varying ripeness, including red and white nandina, Chinese photinia, and green holly berries. All are colors seen in the Duke of Gloucester dinnerware. A gilded star anise is placed on the top of each tree. Bud vases with sweetheart roses, berries, and Leyland cypress sprigs also pick up the colors of the china.

How to Make a Garland Using Foam-Filled Cages

Colorful garlands hang from sconces on either side of the mantel. They add a holiday look using lady apples, kumquats, cranberries, multiflora and rugosa rose hips, sprigs of boxwood, Alexandrian laurel, variegated ivy, and assorted photinia, nandina, and pyracantha berries. They can be made longer or shorter by adjusting the following instructions and using different plant materials. You can also use dried materials. When setting a Christmas table, select fruits, flowers, berries, and/or foliage whose colors look best with your china.

Supplies and materials needed: Eight $4^3/4$ x $1^3/4$ x $^7/8$ inch instant deluxe floral foam sections, four 6 x 2 inch cylindrical green plastic interlocking cages, two 25-inch straight pieces of coat hanger wire, #26 gauge green floral wire, six 20-inch strands of heavy gold cording taped at the ends to prevent fraying, conditioned plant materials (see page 206), 3-inch floral picks, wooden toothpicks, and wired gold ribbon.

Cut the floral foam sections to fit the cages and then soak them in water.

Make a loop at one end of each section of the coat hanger wire for the tops of the garlands. Use the floral wire to secure three strands of cording to the top of each piece. Simultaneously twist the three strands of cording diagonally around the coat hanger wire while pushing the strands together to completely conceal it. Secure the cording at the bottom of the coat hanger wire with the floral wire. Leave 3 inches of the remaining cording below the end of the coat hanger wire.

Open each cage and wedge a strip of the wet floral foam into both sides. Work with both pieces of the coat hanger wire wrapped with the cording at the same time to ensure both pairs of cages will be identical in size. Place a wrapped wire with the loop at the top on each set of cages. Wrap an additional 3-inch piece of floral wire around the hook at the top of the closed cage and turn tightly around the wrapped wire to secure the cage more firmly to the wrapped wire.

Remember to allow about 2¹/₂ inches between the two cages so the plant materials will not appear to merge. Leaving sufficient space will allow the cording to show between the two cages. When the spacing between each section of two cages is similar, close the cage so the wrapped wire is centered between the two pieces of floral foam. Wire each section closed with a 3-inch piece of floral wire with the ends twisted together. The two sections should be identical.

To decorate with the plant materials, start with short boxwood sprigs, 3 to 4 inches long with the bottom leaves removed. Fan the pieces around the front and side edges and cover with boxwood to completely conceal the mechanics. On the ends use 1-inch pieces inserted at an angle to cover the mechanics but not the cord. Do not add plant materials to the backs. They should lie flat against the wall.

Impale the lady apples or other pieces of fruit on the floral picks. Vary the placement of the picks in the fruit. Insert the fruit at different angles into the foam to establish a random arrangement. Add the smaller fruits and berries by impaling them on toothpicks or floral wire and inserting them into the foam. Scatter the fruits and berries over the four sections for a balanced design. Add sprigs of Alexandrian laurel, with the bottom leaves removed, and variegated ivy to give contrasting textures, shapes, and colors. The butterflies and other insects used here replicate those on the dinnerware.

Hang the two garlands side by side when decorating them to help keep them symmetrical. When they are completed, mist well and attach them to the sconces. Separate the strands of the cording below the coat hanger wire to create a tassel at the bottom of each garland. Add a wired gold ribbon bow to conceal the mechanics at the top where each is attached.

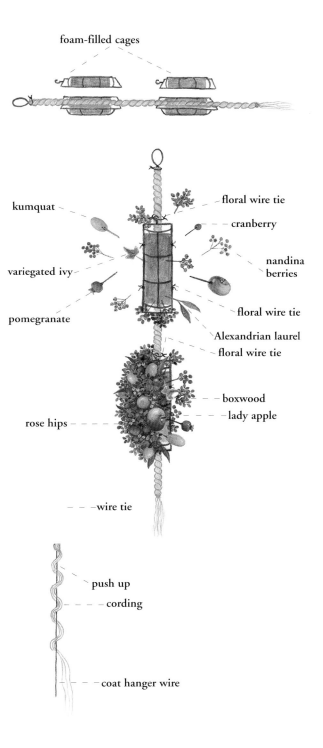

foam-filled cages

kumquat

floral wire tie

cranberry

variegated ivy

nandina berries

pomegranate

floral wire tie

Alexandrian laurel

floral wire tie

boxwood

lady apple

rose hips

wire tie

push up

cording

coat hanger wire

99

How to Make a Swag Using Foam-Filled Cages

Make this decoration using the same plastic cages, available from your floral supplier, listed on page 98. In this version, several cages are used to form two swags centered below the eighty-seven-inch-long mantel. Use an additional cage on each end and one in the middle to form the drops. The wet floral foam allows fresh flowers or other fresh plant materials to be used in a different and elegant manner. You can add dried accents. You can also adapt this decoration for any width fireplace, above an archway, around a column, or along a railing.

Supplies and materials needed: Fresh and dried materials such as small dried pomegranates, cones, nandina berry sprays, multiflora rose hips, walnuts, and Siberian iris pods, gold paint pen, awl, water-resistant glue, 3-inch wooden picks, synthetic sponge, scrap of wood, drill with small bit, #18 gauge green floral wire, seventeen 6 x 2 inch cylindrical green plastic interlocking cages, seventeen instant deluxe floral foam sections 4³/₄ x 1³/₄ x 1³/₄ inches, conditioned plant materials (see page 206), wired gold silk ribbon, and #26 gauge green paddle wire.

Gild the walnuts and the tips of the iris pods with a gold paint pen. Make a small hole in each pome-

Opposite: A thirty-inch fir balsam wreath hangs above the mantel. A Neapolitan-style angel, dressed in gossamer silks and holding an antique sensor, is suspended nearby. Sprigs of white pine, variegated holly, Indian hawthorn, and Alexandrian laurel add lightness and variety to the wreath. Dried pomegranates, gilded iris pods, nandina berries, and white pinecones are inserted into the wreath and repeat the materials used in the swag below.

granate with an awl and glue a 3-inch wooden pick in the hole. Vary the placement of the picks so the pomegranates can be placed at different angles. Let the glue dry thoroughly. Place each walnut on the sponge on top of the piece of scrap wood (to protect your work surface) and drill through the base of the walnut into the sponge. The sponge will help hold the walnut steady. Thread an 8-inch piece of floral wire through both holes. Twist the ends of the floral wire together at the base. These ends will be inserted into the floral foam.

Open each cage and wedge a piece of the wet floral foam into the holder. Install each swag before filling the cages with plant materials. Seven cages have been hooked together and used on each side of the mantel. To hang the swags, hammer nails carefully in the corners of the mantel and between pieces of the moldings, angled away from the mantel. When the nails are removed, the holes can be filled with soap if they show. Make four wire loops from 10-inch lengths of the floral wire. Attach a loop to each end of the first swag and hang the loops over the nails. Repeat with the second swag. The cages should be about 4 inches away from the nails. Insert sprigs of boxwood into the cages starting at the center of the mantel with the foliage pointing toward the center. The floral foam may drip when the plant materials are added, so protect your flooring or hearth until the dripping stops. Continue to add the boxwood, overlapping the ends until the two swags are covered on the fronts and sides. Do not cover the backs of the cages. Add sprigs of white pine to give a soft texture, then follow with sprigs of Alexandrian laurel, variegated ivy, and Indian hawthorn foliage all facing the same direction as the boxwood. Both sides should contain approximately the same amount and variety of plant materials so they are symmetrical. The effect should be light and airy.

Insert the pomegranates into the floral foam, varying the angles but making sure they are spaced evenly on each of the two sections and are orientated toward the center. Insert the nandina berries, rose hips,

walnuts, and iris pods. Add fresh flowers such as white freesia and paper-white narcissus, cutting their stems short. The wet floral foam will help them to stay fresh for several days. Continue to insert freesia and paper-white narcissus alternately into the foam, facing the center. Stand back and see what needs to be added or subtracted to give a harmonious balance.

Attach a wire loop to two cages and hang them on the existing nails at each end of the mantel. Select two similar long pieces of Alexandrian laurel and place them in the lower ends of each cage. Add some white pine for delicacy. Insert long sprigs of nandina berries, iris pods, and white pinecones on picks. Tuck in

boxwood sprigs, a grouping of three pomegranates, a walnut or two, and paper-white narcissus blooms and buds. The two drops should be symmetrical. Place the plant materials in the center cage facing down, but keep this cage shorter than the side groupings for a graceful look. Omit the pinecones from the center drop to keep it looking more delicate. Fasten ribbon bows with pieces of paddle wire to the nails. They will bring an elegant touch and will lighten the corners of the design.

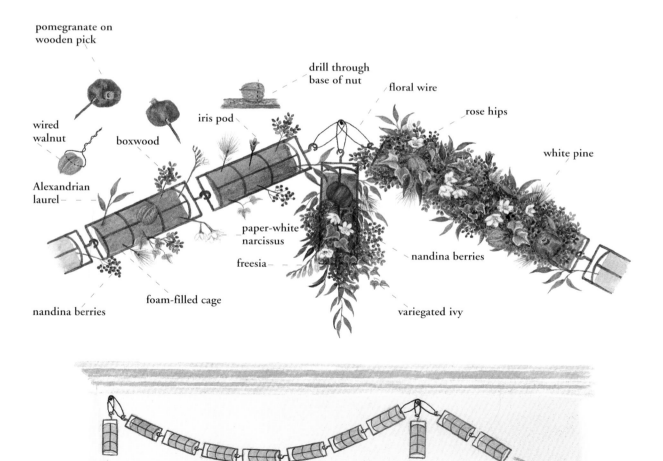

pomegranate on wooden pick

drill through base of nut

floral wire

rose hips

iris pod

white pine

wired walnut

boxwood

Alexandrian laurel

paper-white narcissus

freesia

nandina berries

nandina berries

foam-filled cage

variegated ivy

To prepare a wreath for hanging, determine the distance you want it to hang from the fixture, then measure and cut four pieces of strong ribbon. Leave enough ribbon to wrap around the wreath and the fixture on which you are hanging it. Tie one end of the ribbons to the wreath. You can add dried cockscomb, pomegranates, fresh Chinese photinia berries, sprigs of incense cedar, variegated aucuba, boxwood, and Alexandrian laurel to a large balsam wreath to give it color and texture. After adding these plant materials, push the candleholder picks evenly into the thickest area of the wreath. Gather and tie the ends of the ribbons and hang the wreath.

An unusual oval wreath of frasier fir is ringed with dried pearly everlasting accented with holly berries and a pineapple arranged on a bed of sweet bay and magnolia leaves and lady apples.

Encircled with cedar sprigs, cotton pods, cinnamon sticks, and yarrow, a popular Williamsburg bird bottle also has a tiny wreath around its opening.

This striking white pine wreath is made with oyster shells, pomegranates, dried artichokes, bittersweet sprigs, and trumpet vine pods.

A classic Williamsburg wreath uses native plants in a creative combination of oranges, lady apples, cotton pods, cut cones, holly berries, and a pineapple on a bed of rosemary.

HOLIDAY DINNER FOR TWO

After entertaining a house full of family and friends on Christmas day, an intimate dinner will restore your equilibrium. Perhaps a small table decoration is in order. This one is made with embroidery hoops set on the base of an antique egg boiler, but it can be done using a small bowl or a stand or any container with sides deep enough to hold the floral foam and floral pins. You can use any of the suggestions from the drawing on page 111.

GRILLED TENDERLOIN OF PORK WITH CRANBERRY AND ORANGE SAUCE

6 to 8 servings

1/4 cup soy sauce
1 tablespoon Dijon mustard
1 tablespoon lemon juice
2 pork tenderloins (about 2 pounds)
4 5-inch rosemary sprigs

Combine the soy sauce, mustard, and lemon juice, and mix well. Place the tenderloins in a plastic bag with this mixture and the rosemary sprigs, and marinate overnight. Oil a grill rack and preheat the grill. Place the tenderloins on the rack, brushing them with some of the marinade left in the plastic bag, and grill 10 minutes, turning once. Coat the tenderloins with any marinade that remains, and grill for about 15 minutes more, turning once, until the meat is done. Serve the tenderloins with the heated cranberry and orange sauce.

CRANBERRY AND ORANGE SAUCE

1 1/2 cups cranberries
3 tablespoons Grand Marnier
3 tablespoons orange marmalade
1/2 teaspoon ground ginger
1 cup orange juice
1 rosemary sprig

Combine the cranberries, Grand Marnier, marmalade, ginger, orange juice, and rosemary. Bring to a boil, then reduce the heat and cook until thickened, stirring frequently.

CRÈME BRÛLÉE WITH LAVENDER JELLY

6 servings

3 cups heavy cream
10 tablespoons and 12 teaspoons sugar, divided
1 tablespoon lavender blossoms
1 1/2 teaspoons vanilla

2 whole eggs
3 egg yolks
salt
cinnamon
6 teaspoons lavender jelly

Preheat the oven to 300°F. Scald the cream and 3 tablespoons of sugar. Allow the mixture to cool slightly. Add the lavender blossoms and vanilla, steep for 20 minutes, and strain through a fine sieve. Whisk the eggs and egg yolks with 7 tablespoons sugar and a pinch of salt. Slowly whisk in the cooled cream mixture. Pour the custard mixture into shallow gratin dishes or ramekins that hold slightly more than $1/2$ cup. Shake a bit of cinnamon on the tops. Place the custards into a baking pan and place it in the oven. Pour water into the baking pan about halfway up the sides of the dishes. Bake at 300°F. approximately 35 minutes or until the custards are set. Remove them from the oven, cool on a rack, then place them in the refrigerator covered with plastic wrap. Before serving, sprinkle 2 teaspoons of sugar on top of each chilled custard and caramelize with a blowtorch, with a salamander, or in the oven under the broiler until the sugar is evenly browned. Add 1 teaspoon lavender jelly on top of each custard.

HILDEGARD'S NERVE COOKIES
300 cookies

Hildegard of Bingen was a twelfth-century German abbess whose spiritual songs and recipes with curative powers are still enjoyed today. Soothe your nerves, as did her followers, with these paper-thin cookies.

$1^{1}/2$ cups butter
3 cups brown sugar
2 eggs, well beaten
6 cups flour, divided
4 teaspoons baking powder
$1/2$ teaspoon salt
$1/2$ teaspoon cloves
$2^{1}/4$ teaspoons cinnamon
$2^{1}/4$ teaspoons nutmeg
1 cup almonds, chopped or ground (optional)

Cream the butter and sugar until light and fluffy. Add the eggs. Sift 5 cups of the flour with the baking powder, salt, cloves, cinnamon, and nutmeg, and add to the creamed mixture. Knead in the remaining flour. Add the almonds if desired. Form into 2 x 8 inch rolls, wrap in waxed paper, and chill thoroughly. When firm, preheat the oven to 375°F. Cut the rolls into very thin slices and bake on ungreased cookie sheets at 375°F. until slightly brown. **Note:** This dough freezes well, so make only as many cookies as you will need at one time.

How to Make a Holiday Decoration with Embroidery Hoops

Supplies and materials needed: Wire cutters, #18 gauge floral wire, white glue, dried thyme, gold paint pen, six cedar berries, six tiny cherubs, 5-inch-tall container, two 8-inch wooden embroidery hoops, #26 gauge spool wire, green sheet moss, invisible sewing thread, instant deluxe floral foam, floral pins, long string of tiny gold beads, red nandina berries, and conditioned plant materials (see page 206).

Cut six pieces of floral wire and bend them into tiny hearts for the cherubs to hold. Using white glue, cover them with dried thyme. Allow the hearts to dry, then highlight with touches of gold. Glue a cedar berry onto each heart. When it is dry, glue the gilded hearts to the cherubs.

Select a container and embroidery hoops that will be complementary in size. Insert the outer hoop inside the inner hoop at a right angle to divide the hoops equally and to create an oval shape. Secure the top and bottom crossing points with the spool wire. Use dampened sheet moss secured by wrapping invisible thread around the moss to cover the form (see page 207 for coloring sheet moss). Stand the hoops on newspaper to dry.

Soak the floral foam, cut it to fit into the container, and cover with moss. Secure the hoops in the foam with floral pins. Hang three of the cherubs with invisible thread, facing out from the top of the hoops at different heights. Attach the other three cherubs to the sides of the hoops. Tie the string of gold beads to a floral pin and anchor the pin in the foam under a hoop. Wind the beads around the frames at similar intervals until all the surfaces are garlanded. Tie the end of the string of beads onto a floral pin and insert it under the hoop you have just covered. Tuck 1-inch sprigs of red nandina berries under the beads on the outsides of the hoops.

Push short sprigs of variegated osmanthus through the moss into the wet foam to cover the moss. Add small clumps of nandina berries. Insert a small white spray rose into the foam at the base of each hoop on the outside edge. Water periodically to keep the roses, foliage, and moss fresh.

This container is quite formal. Less formal possibilities are below. Other objects could be used with this type of formal decoration, such as crystal stars, bells, or tiny angels. You can make a less formal decoration by placing the hoops in a moss-covered flowerpot and hanging tiny garden tools, little bunches of flowers, dragonflies, or other small objects on the wooden hoops. **Note:** The size of the hoops should be in scale with the container you use.

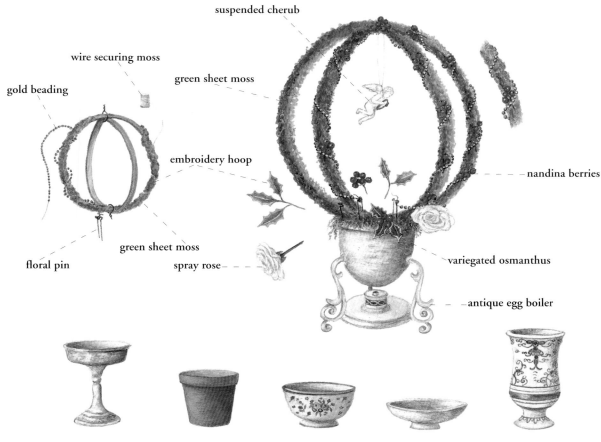

suspended cherub

wire securing moss

gold beading

green sheet moss

embroidery hoop

nandina berries

floral pin

green sheet moss

spray rose

variegated osmanthus

antique egg boiler

other suggested containers

FIVE CHRISTMAS TREE IDEAS

Cutting a tree to bring indoors to decorate with simple handmade ornaments is a German tradition from the nineteenth century. Williamsburg's first recorded Christmas tree was the small one Charles Minnegerode, a German professor at the College of William and Mary, gave his friend and colleague, Nathaniel Beverley Tucker, in 1842 to the delight of Tucker's children.

A Christmas Tree for the Birds

During the Christmas holidays, ask the young naturalists in your family to select a tree outside a window or put one on your deck or terrace and decorate it with fruits and seeds that will attract birds to your yard. In cold months, the tree will give pleasure not only to your family, but also to your feathered guests.

This tree is garlanded with strings of dried apricots and cranberries, dark and golden raisins, and cranberry and popcorn chains. Bunches of millet, assorted berries, thickly cut slices of fresh oranges, apple rings, kumquats, lady apples, grapefruit halves filled with seeds, sunflower heads, suet cakes, miniature corncobs, and pinecones spread with peanut butter mixed with cornmeal and rolled in wild birdseed or peanut halves cover the tree. A star made from dried corncobs tied together with ribbon tops the tree. All decorations are hung with natural garden twine or red ribbon.

Another way to lure birds to your garden in the winter is to plant trees, shrubs, and bushes with berries on which they feed. Holly, crab apple, dogwood

and mountain ash trees, pyracantha, highbush cranberry and other viburnums, winterberry, beautyberry, and Russian olive shrubs and bushes produce berries and seeds that are birds' favorites.

Suet mixed with peanuts, seeds, and raisins, or served plain, is an excellent form of nourishment. Birds will appreciate a source of fresh water on the coldest days of winter. Some birds are ground feeders and will like sand or grit added to the seed. Other birds will come to open feeding trays or to conventional hanging feeders. Bags of thistle seeds attract finches; suet bags, sunflower heads, and bunches of wheat appeal to many birds. Keep the supply constant so birds will bring their friends for you to enjoy. Any of the listed seeds can be used without the suet to fill feeders. Shelled sunflower seeds will prevent damage to the plantings under your feeder. Try one or more of the following recipes.

SUET CAKES

1 cup suet
1 cup peanut butter, raisins, or currants
1 cup wild birdseed
2 cups cornmeal

Cut the suet into small cubes and cook over low heat until melted. Mix in the peanut butter, raisins, or currants, birdseed, and cornmeal. Pour the mixture into flexible, plastic square containers. To make a hole for a hanger, insert a toothpick into each cake, twist several times, and leave until the mixture hardens. Remove the toothpick and bend the container to release the cake. The hole will easily allow you to hang the suet cakes by a ribbon or string or place in wire cages. Be sure the cages are made of coated wire so the birds do not stick to them in freezing weather. You can also put the cakes into plastic onion or lemon bags and tie them onto a tree branch, or hang them from a metal shepherd's crook used in the summer to hold a hummingbird feeder or a hanging plant.

GOLDFINCH TREATS

Williamsburg is home to many kinds of finches and their antics make them worth attracting to your feeder. Special bags with tiny holes are available for thistle seeds to draw in members of the finch family.

1 cup suet
1 cup thistle seed
1 cup sunflower chips
1 cup oil sunflower seeds
1 cup wild birdseed
2 cups cornmeal

Cut the suet into small cubes and cook over low heat until melted. Mix in the thistle seed, sunflower chips, sunflower seeds, birdseed, and cornmeal, and spoon the mixture into a muffin tin lined with paper muffin cups. Insert a toothpick in each to make a hole for hanging. Chill until hardened.

CARDINAL DELIGHTS

Cardinals add bright color to the winter scene. They love sunflower chips, striped sunflower seeds, cracked corn, and white millet. Safflower seeds will help keep the squirrels and grackles away.

1 cup suet
1 cup sunflower chips
1 cup striped sunflower seeds
1 cup white millet
1/2 cup cracked corn
1/2 cup safflower seeds
1 teaspoon sand
green grapes (optional)

Cut the suet into small cubes and cook over low heat until melted. Mix in sunflower chips, sunflower seeds, millet, cracked corn, safflower seeds, and sand. If it seems too dry, add some green grapes cut into small pieces. Line a loaf pan with plastic wrap so the wrap extends over the sides. Fill with the mixture and pack it down. Make three evenly spaced holes with a toothpick for hanging. Chill the mixture until hardened. Pull the block out of the container by lifting the plastic wrap, and cut into three cakes.

How to Make a Corncob Star

Supplies and materials needed: Five large, similarly sized dried ears of corn, 2 yards of flexible coated clothesline wire, and 2 yards of ribbon.

Assemble the ears of corn on a flat surface in a star shape. Holding the end of the clothesline wire in one hand, wind the wire securely around the first ear about one-third of the distance from its base. Bring the wire under the back of the cob to the next ear of corn. Continue to wind the wire around the ears so they are evenly spaced and secured. Twist the wire end to the remaining wire. Continue the same process with the ribbon and tie the two ends on the back. Bend the remaining wire and use it to fasten the star to a treetop. The branches on the tree will also help hold the star in place. Now watch for your visitors.

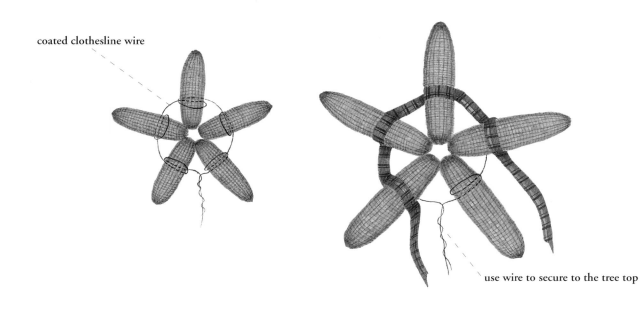

coated clothesline wire

use wire to secure to the tree top

A GARDENER'S CHRISTMAS TREE

A whimsical tree created by a garden lover has some surprises that you can easily make at home. Raffia, garden twine, or crochet thread can turn almost any small object into an ornament. Create ornaments by attaching twine loops to small gardening implements, tiny gloves, plastic insect friends and pests, small baskets of potpourri, papier-mâché vegetables and fruits, small birdhouses, miniature versions of Colonial Williamsburg's bird bottles, beehives, beeswax stars with star anise centers, nests with tiny eggs, and colonial garden helpers pushing wheelbarrows and holding spades. A chain made from circles of cornhusks loops around the tree. Bunches of bright red dried cayenne peppers tied with raffia and the treetop decoration were inspired by peppers grown in colonial days and now cultivated in The Colonial Garden and Nursery and behind King's Arms Tavern. Garden trugs filled with assorted bright primroses, beeskeps, and baskets of fruits and berries on a bright burlap cloth add color under the tree.

Make a beeswax ornament by melting a beeswax block. Pour the hot wax over a four-inch loop of twine anchored with a drop or two of hot wax in the middle of a mold, like the old maple sugar star one used here. Immediately after pouring the wax, add a star anise in the center. Place the mold in the freezer. After the wax chills, it will pull away from the edge of the mold and the star can quickly be released. The loop serves as a hanger.

Dried cornhusks cut into equal strips have been made into a chain reminiscent of the paper ones used on Williamsburg's first Christmas tree. Combine the large and the small on your tree for an added touch of whimsy. Huge paper butterflies and bees contrast with the small scarecrow dressed in colonial garb like the one in the garden behind the James Geddy House and small versions of bird bottles that hang on the front of the Edinburgh Castle Tavern.

On the paper cone is a reminder that rosemary is the herb of remembrance.

How to Make a Treetop Wreath Using Wire

A cayenne pepper ring, backed with camellia leaves and a raffia bow, sits on the treetop. The botanical print of a branch of peppers on the wall beside the tree is reproduced from an original seventeenth-century one in Colonial Williamsburg's collection.

Supplies and materials needed: Latex gloves, fresh cayenne peppers, clippers, #18 gauge green floral wire, pliers, scissors, heavy cardboard, camellia or other

118

glossy conditioned leaves (see page 206), masking tape, #22 gauge green floral wire, and raffia.

Wearing latex gloves, gather the peppers. If they are on branches, cut the peppers, leaving short stems. Thread each pepper through the middle using the #18 gauge floral wire, with some headed in, some out, some up, and some down to give dimension to the wreath. Keep threading the peppers onto the wire, pushing them together to pack them as tightly as possible, until you can curve the wreath to the correct size for the top of your tree. Join the curved ends and twist them with pliers to tighten and hold the wreath securely.

Cut a donut-shaped ring from the cardboard and place the pepper wreath on top, making sure that the cardboard base does not show on the inside of the wreath. Stack the leaves and cut off their stem ends. Tape the cut tip ends of the leaves to the cardboard so the leaves slightly overlap and form an attractive band around the outside of the wreath. You can also add an

additional border of leaves around the inside edge that will show if you are making a large wreath of peppers. Cut two 8-inch pieces of #22 gauge floral wire and bend each into a hairpin shape. Poke both ends of each hairpin through the wreath and through the two small holes in the cardboard at the top and bottom. Twist the ends together at the back of the cardboard to secure them. The peppers and leaves will conceal the wire. You can prop it up in the highest branches, or you can wire it in place. Use the heavier wire to attach the wreath to the tree. Gather several strands of raffia and tie them into a bow. Trim as needed and wire the bow on the wreath.

You may need to add another piece of #18 gauge floral wire if you are making a wreath larger than this 8-inch one. For a larger, thicker, and wider wreath, thread each pepper about one-third of its length, heading some in and some out. Allow the peppers to face up as well as toward the inside and outside. **Note:** You can also use wire to make a wreath out of any pod-shaped material.

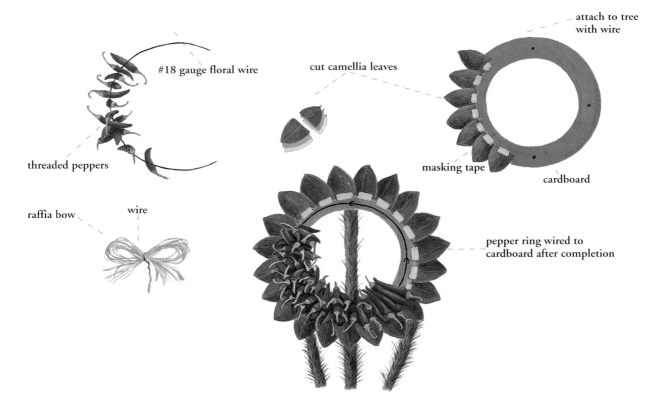

#18 gauge floral wire

cut camellia leaves

attach to tree
with wire

threaded peppers

masking tape

cardboard

raffia bow   wire

pepper ring wired to
cardboard after completion

A HOTCH POTCH CHRISTMAS TREE

These engaging fellows are adapted from *The Comical HOTCH-POTCH, or the ALPHABET turn'd POSTURE-MASTER,* a print sold by Carington Bowles, first issued in London in 1782. Mr. Hotch Potch entertained and instructed, as many of today's toys do. The popular Hotch Potch toys reproduced by Colonial Williamsburg here are gardeners who climb about this tree picking small lady apples from the branches. Some sport butterfly nets while others lounge casually under the tree, resting after their active day. The tree is trimmed with alphabet cookies, wooden letters, Hotch Potch alphabet cards made into ornaments, and a chain of apricots and cranberries. At the top of the large tree is a cookie star.

COOKIE TREETOP STAR

1 cup sugar, divided
$^1/2$ cup butter
3 eggs
1 teaspoon anise
$2^1/2$ cups all-purpose flour
salt

Obtain a nested set of plastic star-shaped cookie cutters with wide top edges (there are usually six cutters in a set) or three heavy cardboard stars of decreasing size. Preheat the oven to 375°F. Grease a cookie sheet. Cream $^3/4$ cup sugar with the butter. Mix 2 eggs with the anise and stir into the sugar-butter mixture. Sift the flour and a pinch of salt and combine with the sugar-butter mixture. Chill the dough until stiff, then roll it out to a $^1/2$-inch thickness. Beginning with the largest star, use every other one. Take the wide upper

edge of the largest cutter and press it into the dough to make a deep indentation. Cut out the star by following its outline in the dough, leaving a $^1/2$-inch border. Take the third largest cutter and make a similar indentation. Repeat with the smallest cutter. Beat the remaining egg and paint the raised portions of the star with a thin layer of egg wash. While the star is still damp, sprinkle and press the remaining sugar on the raised dough sections. Place the star on the prepared cookie sheet and bake 10 minutes or until golden. **Note:** Roll out the remaining dough to make Hotch Potch figures or letters that you can ice or paint.

How to Make a Hotch Potch Jumping Jack

Popular nineteenth-century toys, jumping jacks still engage young guests at the Abby Aldrich Rockefeller Folk Art Museum holiday exhibition. This example features Mr. Hotch Potch. You can make it any size by enlarging the pattern.

Supplies and materials needed:
#140 heavy watercolor paper or mat board, scissors or craft knife, assorted paints and brushes, glue, T-pin, needle, two 20-inch pieces of strong, thin linen thread, wire cutters, #28 gauge spool wire, needle-nose pliers, seed beads, fine sewing pins, and a 4 x 6 inch piece of corrugated cardboard.

After enlarging the pattern, trace the components on the paper or mat board and cut out one head and two each of the body, arms, and upper and lower legs. Paint both sides of the arms and legs identically. Then paint the face and back of the head. Finally, paint only one side of each body piece. Glue the neck to the front body piece, then add details to the face.

Transfer the x's and dots from the pattern to your jumping jack pieces. Thread will go through the x's; wire, through the dots. Place the pattern over your pieces and make a hole with a T-pin at the x's and dots on all pieces. Arrange the pieces with feet facing out and hands down.

Thread a needle with the two linen strands. Go down through the x on the front of the left arm and come up through the back of the x of the right arm, leaving two equal tails of thread.

Cut six 2-inch lengths of spool wire. With the pliers or T-pin, make a small curl or twist at one end of each wire.

Create a knee joint by inserting one wire through the two holes in the knee sections of a set of upper and lower leg pieces. With feet facing out, the upper leg piece should be on top of the lower leg piece. Curl the wire on each side so there is a slight looseness or

play at the knee. Repeat for the other leg pieces.

Connect an arm by inserting one wire through the back body piece, then a seed bead, then the dot on the arm, and finally another seed bead. Repeat for the other arm.

Pin your jumping jack to the cardboard for stability before knotting the thread. Position the arms parallel to the body piece and, using the hole the wire has come through, anchor the body piece and arms with sewing pins (through the seed beads if possible) to hold them in place. Tie the two long ends of thread together with a square knot so the strands between the two arms are straight across. Tie a second knot about 3/4 inch from the bottom of the body piece.

Separate the two strands. With a needle, take one strand up through the x on a leg, leaving the tail loose. Repeat with the other leg.

Connect a leg to the body by inserting one wire through the back body piece, then a seed bead, then the dot on the leg, and finally another seed bead. Repeat for the other leg.

Secure the legs with a pin pushed into the cardboard just outside the legs. The feet should still be facing outward. Tie a square knot with the two threads, centered between the legs.

Unpin the jumping jack from the cardboard. Join the front and back body pieces by inserting the four wires through the dots on the front body piece. Curl or twist the wire so all parts are held together securely. Cut the wire with wire cutters. Tie a knot in the thread and trim it to even the ends.

Make a hole in the hat and insert a dark-colored hanger that will not show on the tree. Pull and enjoy your jumping jack.

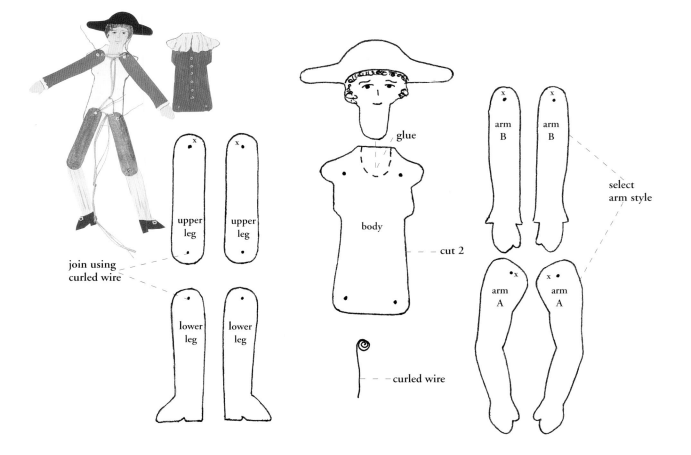

Bright paper cornucopias filled with nandina and tallow berries contrast with the flat felt ornaments and needlework chain on the tree.

A QUILTER'S CHRISTMAS TREE

Flowers from the garden have been motifs for treasured quilts from the past and are still used by modern quilters. Floral designs from an appliquéd cotton quilt top in the Abby Aldrich Rockefeller Folk Art Museum, noted for its collection of quilts and woven coverlets, inspired the ornaments for this tree. Attributed to Theodore Runyon Dunham and Sarah Elizabeth Haines Dunham, the quilt top was probably made between 1870 and 1890. Family history says that Theodore Dunham cut out the intricately shaped pieces and planned the design while his wife carefully hemstitched the appliqués.

Due to the fastness of Turkey red dye, red and white quilts were popular in the nineteenth century and continue to be today. In the photograph of the original quilt *(opposite, above)*, the diagonals of the red sashing form diamond shapes into which the floral motifs have been applied with tiny hemstitches.

How to Make Christmas Ornaments Using Quilt Designs

Supplies and materials needed: Felt in selected colors, medium-weight iron-on bonding agent, iron, plastic sheets or heavy paper, sharp scissors, T-square, needle with large eye, and heavy thread.

Using the following patterns, enlarge the designs (via photocopy) and select two colors. You can create your own designs following these directions.

Divide each color of felt in half. Bond the iron-on agent to one surface of half of both colors of felt. Leave the peel-away paper in place.

Make plastic or heavy paper templates of the patterns, and trace these patterns onto the paper of the bonding material on the color of felt you have selected for the principal color of the design. Cut out the felt designs. Use a T-square to cut squares large enough to include the design and the surrounding border from the contrasting felt, one with bonding material and one without, for each ornament.

Start with a felt square without the bonding agent, remove the paper backing from a cutout design and bond the design onto the center of an unbonded felt square with your iron. Press the strips of felt with the bonding agent on the backs to form a

frame around the design. Position the strips so no spaces are seen once they are ironed in place. Join a square with the bonding material to a square with the design. Press and trim as needed. If you wish to have a design on both sides, bond a second design on the plain back of the ornament.

Add the hanger by running the thread between or parallel to the two pieces of bonded felt, about 1/2-inch from the tip of the square. Cut the thread and tie a knot at the ends. This method ensures that the ornament will hang correctly.

AN ANGEL TREE

Reflecting the colors in the room for which it was designed, an elegant tree features various sizes of angels and cherubs in robes of cream, salmon, and gold silk, gilded pinecones and brass stars, and nosegays, or tussie-mussies, of dried roses (see page 63). Gossamer gold ribbons, twisted slightly when they are placed over the branches to give a billowy effect, and cording encircle the tree.

Tussie-mussies are handheld nosegays that served our ancestors as portable air fresheners. The name comes from the Middle English word "tusmose," derived from "tussock," meaning "wispy," and "mussie," for the moss used to keep the plant material fresh. It is fitting that the angels and cherubs on the tree are surrounded with these small arrangements of roses, traditionally the symbol of purity.

How to Make a Nosegay

Supplies and materials needed: 1 yard of 3-inch-wide cotton lace, small scissors, needle, white thread, three dried roses, dried sprigs of asters or other small dried plant materials (see page 63), and green floral tape.

These nosegays are bordered with lace collars. To make the collar, gather the inside long edge of the lace so there is a 1/2-inch opening in the center. With right sides facing, sew the two narrow ends together with a 1/4-inch seam. Form the dried roses and asters or other dried materials into small nosegays and wrap the wired stems with floral tape. Insert the stems through the center of the lace collar and bend the wire parallel to the collar. Place the nosegays on the branches for support.

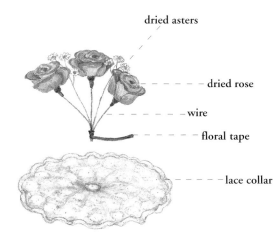

gathers

hem

dried asters

dried rose

wire

floral tape

lace collar

On each side of a large punch bowl encircled with a fruit and evergreen wreath, imposing lady apple cones topped with small pineapples are mounted on urns.

OLD FORMS, NEW WAYS: CONES

The very essence of a Williamsburg Christmas table is the fruit cone on which apples and lemons have been traditionally used mixed with assorted seasonal greenery. You can substitute other fruits to great effect individually or combined. A special effect such as chains of cranberries and kumquats (see page 130) is a new way to embellish this old form.

To make this cone of subtle reds and greens, place a wooden nail-studded form covered with Spanish moss in the center of a container of living variegated ivy and wrap ivy tendrils up and around the cone to cover the surface. Anchor the ends of the tendrils where necessary using four-inch-long wire hairpins made from #18 gauge floral wire. Impale polished red plums and green tomatillos on the nails in a random pattern and nestled in the ivy. Hang bunches of green and red grapes on the hairpins and anchor them under the moss and ivy. Use ivy leaves to soften the shapes of the fruit, and add kalanchoe blossom clusters for contrast.

Muted tones of Seckel pears, small, white spray roses, sprigs of heather, and variegated moonshadow euonymus harmonize with the colors selected for the Christmas wedding in which this decoration was used.

How to Make a Christmas Cone on a Nail-Studded Wooden Cone

Supplies and materials needed: 2¹/₂-inch (8 penny) galvanized finishing nails, 10-inch nail-studded wooden cone form (a 7-inch and a 10-inch cone are available through Colonial Williamsburg), Spanish moss, 8-inch cardboard round, lemons in varying sizes, 1-inch wire nails, needle-nose pliers, #20 gauge green floral wire, kumquats, cranberries, wire cutters,

The sugaring of the variety of green fruits used in this cone softens its colors.

hook to secure garland

wooden cone

row of added nails

wire nail hook

Spanish moss

cranberry and kumquat
garland on wire

cardboard round

pineapple top

lemon

cedar

conditioned plant materials (see page 206), clippers, a pineapple with a symmetrical and unblemished top, and a decorative plate.

Hammer rows of additional finishing nails between the existing nails on the form, angling them up, to better secure the fruit. Cover the cone with Spanish moss to conceal the form. Place it on the cardboard round.

Take the smallest lemons and see how many will fit around the top when placed at an angle. Do not impale the fruit. Usually four lemons will be used, so evenly space four wire nails around the top edge of the cone. Make a C-curve in each nail facing toward the center of the cone with needle-nose pliers. One end of the garland will be attached to this hook. Repeat this process around the base and bend the C-shaped curl away from the cone and slightly down to hold the lower end of the wired garland. Four spirals

of four lemons each will usually fill a 10-inch cone. There should be enough room for the garlands. The largest fruit goes at the bottom of the cone.

To form the first garland, make a small loop at one end of a piece of floral wire. Thread the wire through the length of a kumquat, then two cranberries. Repeat, adding fruit until the garland reaches from the bottom hook in a spiral to the top hook. Trim the wire as needed. Form a pleasing curve to the garland. Make and place the other three garlands in the same manner on the cone. Impale the lemons, spaced evenly, to follow the curves of the garlands. There will be more space between the lemons at the bottom of the form than between those at the top. Continue in this manner around the cone. Anchor cedar sprigs in the Spanish moss between the lemons and under the garlands for more color contrast.

Cut off the pineapple top, impale it on the top nail, and tuck cedar sprigs around the base.

Fruit and flower cones and tiny topiaries create golden focal points for the table.

NEW YEAR'S EVE DINNER AT THE LIGHTFOOT HOUSE

For a formal New Year's Eve dinner in the Lightfoot House, traditional forms associated with Colonial Williamsburg are seen here in fresh, new ways, with fruits and flowers joined in unexpected combinations.

The decorations accentuate the colors of the dining room's magnificent hand-painted Chinese wallpaper and the green and gold Christmas plates. On the table, two large cones of oranges, kumquats, holly sprigs, and yellow Ducat roses are crowned with pineapples, Virginia's symbol of hospitality since colonial days. Floral foam was used as the base for the cones to prolong the freshness of the roses. The small cones are constructed on plastic, igloo-shaped floral foam forms using kumquats, boxwood sprigs, and miniature pineapples. Miniature boxwood topiaries studded with kumquats are also made on this same versatile form.

A marble serving table holds a bold arrangement of white Virginia roses, Star-of-Bethlehem, miniature pineapples on long stalks, and kumquat rings. To form these rings, the kumquats have been threaded lengthwise on floral wire and bent to form circles. They are attached to long wooden picks, which are inserted into the floral foam. White pine, Leyland cypress, variegated aucuba, and noble fir are the luxuriant base for the fruit and flowers.

The dining table is set for a holiday dessert with air twist goblets, Queen Anne silverware, and green and gold Christmas plates.

This grand room calls for a large and spectacular arrangement. *Opposite:* A close-up of the ring of kumquats also shows the Star-of-Bethlehem, white Virginia roses, miniature ornamental pineapples, and a variety of foliage.

How to Make a Fruit and Flower Cone Using Floral Foam

Supplies and materials needed: Two blocks of instant deluxe floral foam, low 10-inch-wide container with a shallow lip, four 8-inch-long bamboo skewers, serrated knife, large oranges, 8-inch floral picks, conditioned plant materials including American holly, Leyland cypress, and magnolia leaves (see page 206), clippers, Ducat roses, wire cutters, #18 gauge green floral wire, kumquats, and a pineapple.

Soak the floral foam blocks and place them upright in a shallow container. Connect them with the skewers inserted at different angles. Trim off the up-per corners with a knife to taper the top and give it a cone shape. Impale the oranges on floral picks and insert them around the base of the cone at different angles. Do not place them in an even line. Extend the oranges at the base well outside the floral foam. Insert the ones above the base more deeply into the foam. Place the oranges on the top close to the foam. Tapering the placement of the oranges will establish the line of the arrangement.

Fill in the spaces between the oranges with holly and Leyland cypress sprigs, leaving their stems long enough to go into the wet foam. Cut the stems of the roses on the diagonal and long enough to be inserted into the foam. Cut different lengths of floral wire and impale the kumquats on them. Place them at random to give the cone its final outline.

Secure a beautiful pineapple with balanced foliage using floral picks inserted into the top of the cone. Tuck a trimmed band of magnolia leaves and Leyland cypress sprigs under the oranges around the base of the cone.

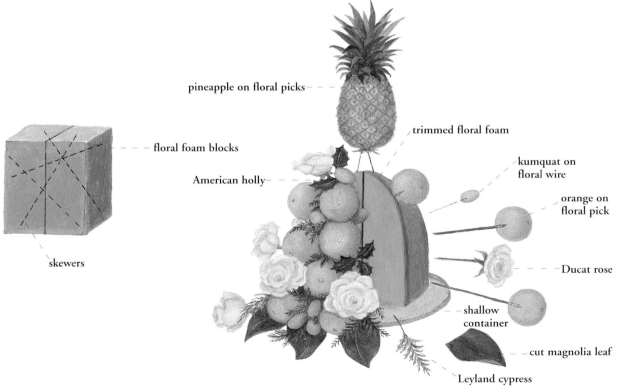

pineapple on floral picks

floral foam blocks

American holly

skewers

trimmed floral foam

kumquat on floral wire

orange on floral pick

Ducat rose

shallow container

cut magnolia leaf

Leyland cypress

The exotic bird on the Chinese wallpaper appears to be taking a nibble from the topiary before trying a taste of the miniature cone below.

How to Make a Miniature "Faux" Topiary Using an Igloo-Shaped Floral Foam Form

You can make small topiaries and cones using an igloo-shaped floral foam form. The tiny topiary *(above)* was used as a place favor for a formal dinner in the magnificent eighteenth-century Lightfoot House where dignitaries stay during their visits to Colonial Williamsburg.

Supplies and materials needed: Decorative container, plastic liner, masking tape, plaster of paris, stirrer, 8-inch stick pointed at one end, gravel, 3¼-inch-tall plastic, igloo-shaped floral foam form, conditioned boxwood sprigs (see page 206), wooden toothpicks, kumquats, and green sheet moss.

Select a decorative container suitable for the size of the small topiary you are making and a plastic liner that will fit inside it. Tape over any drainage holes with masking tape. Fill the liner almost to the top with plaster of paris. Add water and stir quickly. Add more water or plaster of paris as needed and thoroughly mix the ingredients until the plaster of paris is smooth and thick. Push the blunt end of the stick to the bottom of the liner, checking that it is centered and vertical. Let the plaster of paris dry for at least 24 hours, then place the liner into the outer container. Using a removable liner for the form will free this container for other uses. Add gravel to anchor the liner in the container if necessary.

Soak the form, remove the plastic base, invert the foam, and then push the small end down onto the stick about 3 inches. Cover the form with 3- to 4-inch sprigs of boxwood. Insert toothpicks into the stem end of the kumquats and push them into the foam at random. They will look like tiny, round oranges. Cover the surface of the liner with dampened green sheet moss (see page 207). Place a kumquat on the moss for added color.

How to Make a Miniature Cone Using an Igloo-Shaped Floral Foam Form

Supplies and materials needed: 3¼-inch-tall plastic, igloo-shaped floral foam form, kumquats, wooden toothpicks, 2- to 3-inch ornamental pineapple, and conditioned boxwood sprigs (see page 206).

To make a cone approximately 7½ inches tall on the same igloo-shaped floral foam form used for the miniature "faux" topiary, soak the foam in water. Do not remove the plastic base. Divide the kumquats by size. Insert toothpicks in the sides of the largest kumquats and place a row of them around the base with the stem ends facing upward. Add two more rows of kumquats to cover the form. Place the pineapple on the top of the form. Tuck tiny sprigs of boxwood between the kumquats and around the base.

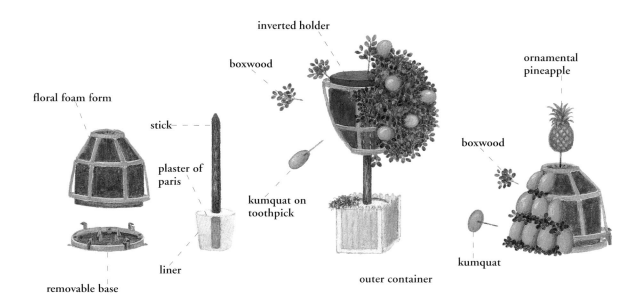

floral foam form · stick · plaster of paris · liner · removable base · boxwood · inverted holder · kumquat on toothpick · outer container · ornamental pineapple · boxwood · kumquat

USING PRESERVED MATERIALS IN WINTER

Plant materials picked from your summer garden and preserved (see pages 62–67) are ready to be used for winter decorations. On the large dining room table at the St. George Tucker House, a tray of preserved materials is arranged on crossed ribbons. "Faux" pineapples are combined with commercially freeze-dried oranges and artichokes, dehydrated orange slices, and nuts (see page 67). Magnolia leaves preserved with glycerine (see page 65) and air-dried okra pods and floral materials (see page 66) have also been used.

How to Make a "Faux" Pineapple

Supplies and materials needed: 10-inch cube of Styrofoam, sharp knife, sheet moss, floral pins, four to six large pinecones, clippers, glue gun or thick white glue, leaves such as bay leaves, star anise leaves, or other long-pointed leaves that will stay green when dried, and #24 gauge floral wire.

Cut the block of Styrofoam with a sharp knife so the base is rounded and tapers slightly toward the top. Hollow out a 1-inch-deep section at the top of the form. Cover the form with sheet moss, attaching it to the Styrofoam using floral pins.

Cut the scales off the pinecones. Starting at the top of the form, take a scale with its rounded end facing up, and attach it with a glue gun or thick white glue to the moss. Continue gluing the scales in overlapping rings around the form moving down to the base. When the form is covered, gather a bunch of leaves, wrap their ends with the floral wire, and glue them into the hole in the top. Attach a few more leaves to 4-inch pieces of floral wire and insert them in the center of the leaves you have glued to give height to the top of the pineapple.

PYRAMIDS

Pyramids were used in the homes of wealthy Virginians in the eighteenth century. They usually included footed glasses containing wine jellies and small dishes of preserved lemon and orange peels and other sweetmeats.

How to Decorate a Pyramid

Matching handblown, tiered glass pyramids are reflected on either side of a handsome antique mirror. Wreaths, in graduated sizes, of variegated holly, Leyland cypress, boxwood, and yellow Rumba roses tinged with red are interspersed with soft, fuzzy skinned yellow trifoliate oranges and blueberries. The blueberries and oranges are impaled on floral wire or toothpicks that have been inserted into floral foam wreath forms. The contrast of textures and colors lends interest to these pyramid arrangements.

Supplies and materials needed: Three 8-inch floral foam wreath forms, sharp serrated knife, a stacking three-tiered glass pyramid, conditioned plant materials (see page 206), Rumba roses, trifoliate oranges, blueberries, toothpicks or 3-inch pieces of #18 gauge green floral wire, goblet, and floral foam.

Cut one of the wreath forms into two half circles to use on the bottom tier leaving 1 1/2 inches between the cut ends. Cut out wedges from the second wreath form and push together to use on the top tier. Leave one ring uncut to go on the middle tier. Soak all the sections in water for 2 hours and then place them on the pyramid. Use 3-inch pieces of boxwood, with bottom leaves stripped, to form a full base for each tier of the decoration. Insert the pieces of boxwood all at the same angle, which will give better coverage and look well. On the bottom tier, carefully fill in the gaps with slightly longer pieces of boxwood and other plant materials. Next add the roses. Leave 2-inch stems on the roses, cut them at an angle, and place them in each tier, leaving space for other plant materials. Impale the trifoliate oranges and blueberries on toothpicks or pieces of floral wire and insert them into the wreaths. Add sprigs of variegated holly and Leyland cypress for a variety of textures. Place a goblet in the

center of the top tier with a small piece of wet foam in it. Put small sprigs of boxwood between the foam and the glass to conceal the foam. Insert holly, cypress, and a few roses in the foam. **Note:** If you place this arrangement against a mirror, make sure the reflected side is balanced with the front side.

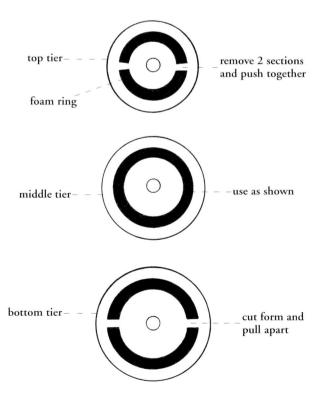

This attractive tiered pyramid was made by stacking two glass cake stands of diminishing sizes. A glass candlestick was inverted to use at the top. Five small, red pears were evenly spaced on the bottom tier with lady apples added randomly. Thin slices of dried clementines, boxwood, nandina foliage and berries, and a few cranberries were added for color. Four small crystal glasses filled with cranberries, each topped with a kumquat in which a clove was inserted in the stem end, were placed on the second tier. Small clementines, foliage, and berries were added to complete this tier. The candlestick was secured in the middle of the top tier with wax, and a small pineapple placed in it. The result is a colorful and wonderfully scented arrangement.

Opposite: The three-tiered handblown glass pyramid and goblet, decorated with roses dried in silica gel (see page 63) and air-dried hydrangeas (see page 66), and the Isis china candlesticks and dinnerware are available from Colonial Williamsburg.

A VALENTINE FOR A GARDENER

Two varieties of woven paper hearts, some with pressed flowers added for decoration, bring a touch of spring on Valentine's Day. The hearts are displayed on a garden trellis surrounded with red and white cyclamen and maidenhair ferns.

These hearts show you how to use traditional crafts to create valentine keepsakes. Hearts inspired by ancient Scandinavian examples, made by interweaving two pieces of paper that have been cut in an identical pattern, are still popular today to give as gifts and as decorations on Christmas trees. By varying the spaces, you can make different patterns, some resembling coverlet designs. They can be made large or small.

Woven heart-and-hand love tokens and valentines, first brought by German settlers to America, also hang on the trellis *(opposite)*. Some were quite elaborate and creative, depending on the skills of the maker. Even today, these mementos are found tucked away in old books and albums. Many of these valentines have verses written on them. A charming one says: "Heart and hand shall never part/when this you see remember me." Consider using this sentiment on a valentine keepsake you make, or pen your own.

How to Make a Scandinavian Woven Heart

Supplies and materials needed: Medium-weight glazed wrapping papers, pen or pencil for marking, patterns in size desired, ruler, scissors, and white glue.

Cut two rectangles of paper of different colors, each three times longer than wide. The smallest example here is 6 x 2 inches. Fold each piece in half with the colored side facing inside to produce two connected sections 3 x 2 inches.

Overlap the two pieces with the folded edges at right angles to one another. Mark a reference line a little wider than the width of the overlapping paper on each folded piece that will be the line to which you will cut the weaving strips. With a ruler, draw the cutting lines shown on the pattern on each folded section to the reference line. Be careful the cutting lines extend to the reference line. If you cut strips that are too short, it will be difficult to complete the weaving. Cut the weaving strips. Round off the open ends, or tops, into semicircles. Make sure the two folded pieces are identical.

Turn the two pieces of papers so the colors are on the outside.

Place the corners of the folded ends at right angles. To weave the heart, insert strip 1 between folded strip A and push strip 1 through. Then open

strip 1 and insert strip B between folded strip 1. Then insert strip 1 between folded strip C and push strip 1 through. Open strip 1, and insert strip D between folded strip 1. Slide woven strip 1 about 3/4 inch toward the rounded end.

Now alternate the weaving with strip 2. Insert strip A between folded strip 2, then insert strip 2 between folded strip B. Insert strip C between folded strip 2. Finally, insert strip 2 between folded strip D. Repeat these steps for the remaining strips. When using patterns with more strips, alternate the strips each time.

When you have finished weaving the heart, cut a piece of matching paper and glue it on either side for a handle. Fill the heart with candies or small gifts and hang it on a tree or give it to your valentine. **Note:** Try these different patterns *(below)* or others that vary the width of the strips. One of the patterns here is from a detail in an antique coverlet in the Abby Aldrich Rockefeller Folk Art Museum. If you cut fine strips, as in two of these examples, slightly extend the length of the weaving strips.

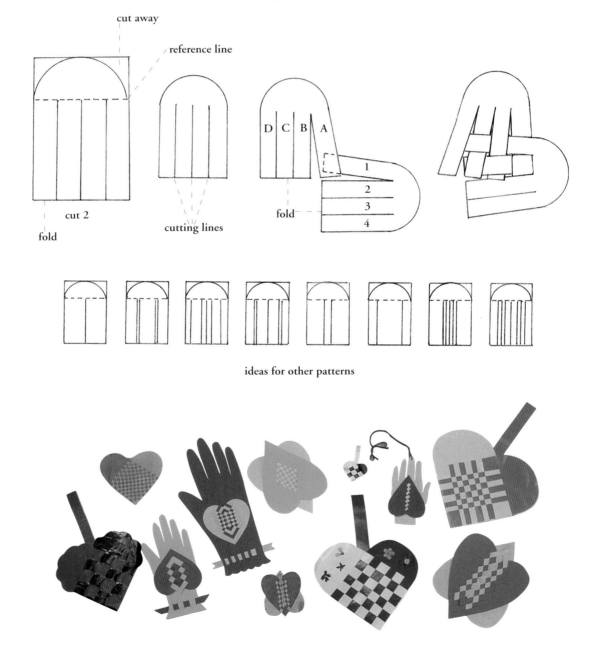

ideas for other patterns

How to Make a Woven Heart-and-Hand and Interwoven Hearts

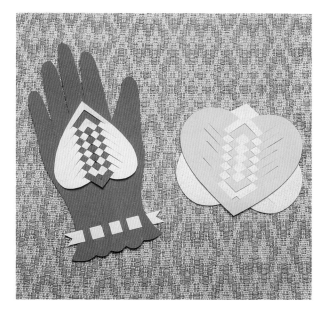

The same steps are followed to weave a heart-and-hand or two interwoven hearts. Usually, the patterns on the two pieces are identical but inverted. Here the series of Vs point upward on the top piece and are reversed on the bottom piece. You can embellish the patterns with punched holes, wristbands, or elaborately cut hearts.

Supplies and materials needed: Patterns, contrasting colors of medium-weight paper of good quality, sharp pencil, ruler, scissors, small cutting mat, and craft knife.

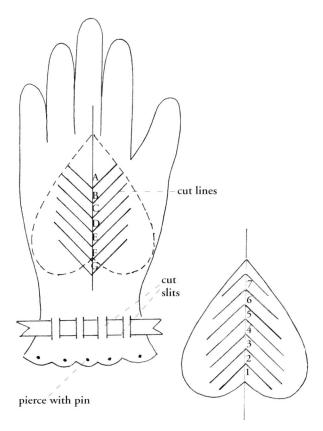

cut lines

cut slits

pierce with pin

Enlarge the patterns and trace them carefully onto the paper. Cut the outline using scissors. Lightly mark the numbers and letters from the patterns with a pencil and carefully cut the weaving lines with a craft knife. Be sure to cut the lines the length shown.

To weave the heart-and-hand, tuck 1 under G, 2 under F, 3 under E, 4 under D, 5 under C, 6 under B, and 7 under A. Move these two interwoven pieces up as far as possible and align the center lines at top and bottom. Bring 6 over A, 5 over B, 4 over C, 3 over D, 2 over E, and 1 over F. Finally, tuck 5 under A, 4 under B, 3 under C, 2 under D, and 1 under E.

You can add a wristband by cutting the slits on the pattern and weaving a narrow strip in and out.

When weaving two hearts together, invert and lightly mark letters on one of the hearts, as you did on the hand. Mark numbers on the second heart, following the pattern. Move the first woven section up as far as possible. Make sure the two elements are properly aligned before proceeding. Follow the preceding weaving directions.

Another springtime harbinger is a Valentine garden. Seasonal flowers fill a large hand-thrown pot. Sugar cookies with marbleized icing designs hang from the dogwood branch in the center.

How to Make a Valentine Pot Garden

An Olmsted pot garden, planted with many spring Tidewater flowers, is a special valentine for your favorite gardener. Unlike traditional container gardens, Olmsted pot gardens are often combinations of bulbs and potted houseplants to which fresh blooms and foliage are added. These indoor gardens require few supplies, yet careful consideration about where you will place them. This pot garden displays potted primroses and daffodils, cut daffodil blossoms, anemones, and snowdrops in tubes, and ranunculus, iris, nandina foliage, and additional anemones in wet floral foam and small vases. Grape hyacinths, crocuses, and scilla, dug from the garden, are also put in small vases or small plastic bags filled with soil. A small pot with a dogwood branch secured in plaster of paris that features hanging sugar cookies is in the center.

Supplies and materials needed: Wide pot, plastic wrap, dish or coaster, floral foam, small pot with dogwood branch in plaster of paris (see page 72), potted plants, bulbs and other plant materials including cut flowers, plastic sandwich bags, small vases with narrow tops, floral tubes, and dampened sphagnum moss.

If you are using a pot with a hole in the bottom, line it with plastic wrap to prevent leaving a mark on the surface on which it will be placed. Add a dish or coaster for additional protection.

Use wet floral foam to stagger the height of the potted plants and to keep cut blooms and boxwood fresh. Decide on the overall design and distribution of colors. Place the small pot with the dogwood branch, which will be used for hanging the cookies, in the center of the large pot. Arrange the potted plants and bulbs you have selected around it. The bulbs can be contained in soil-filled plastic bags. Insert clumps of cut flowers in floral foam or vases. Blooms with delicate stems should go in floral tubes or small vases. Vary the height to create a more natural-looking garden. Dampen the moss and tuck it around to hide any visible mechanics. Attach the cookies to the branches with heavy thread or narrow ribbon.

Note: You can plant the bulbs in the fall or purchase them commercially in pots.

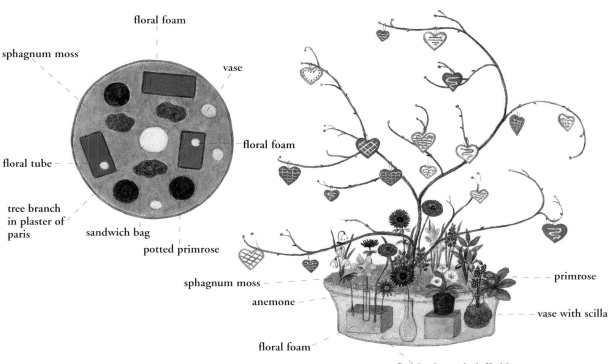

floral foam

sphagnum moss

vase

floral foam

floral tube

tree branch in plaster of paris

sandwich bag

potted primrose

sphagnum moss

anemone

floral foam

floral tube with daffodil

primrose

vase with scilla

SUGAR COOKIES

Six dozen cookies

These cookies are adapted from a recipe for Shrewsbury cakes from Hannah Glasse's 1760 *The Art of Cookery Made Plain and Easy.* They are decorated with patterns inspired by hand-marbleized paper that colonial bookbinders used.

1 cup unsalted butter, softened
1¹/2 cups confectioners' sugar, sifted
1 large egg
1 teaspoon vanilla
2¹/2 cups all-purpose flour
1 teaspoon cream of tartar
1 teaspoon baking soda
¹/4 teaspoon salt
¹/2 teaspoon cinnamon

Cream the butter in a large bowl. Slowly add the sugar and beat until fluffy. Beat in the egg and vanilla. Sift the flour, cream of tartar, baking soda, salt, and cinnamon, stir into the butter mixture, and mix well. Divide the dough into three portions, wrap each in plastic wrap, and chill them in the refrigerator for several hours or overnight. Preheat the oven to 400°F. Grease the baking sheets. Lightly dust a pastry board with confectioners' sugar, roll out one section of the dough, and cut the heart shapes. If you plan to hang the cookies, insert a toothpick into each and leave it in the cookie during baking to form a hole. Bake at 400°F. for 6 to 8 minutes or until lightly colored. While the cookies are still warm, rotate the toothpicks and remove them carefully. Cool the cookies on a rack.

ICING FOR MARBLEIZING

3 egg whites
1 box (1 pound) confectioners' sugar
$1/2$ teaspoon cream of tartar
lemon juice
food coloring

Beat the egg whites with the sugar and cream of tartar on low speed until well mixed. Beat at high speed until thick. Divide the icing into small bowls based on the number of colors you will be using. The icing must be soft to spread easily and to pipe. If it seems too thick, add lemon juice to thin it. Add the food coloring in small amounts until you have the desired colors. Cover the bowls with plastic wrap when you are not using particular icing colors. Select one color and spread the icing evenly over several cookies with a small spatula. Fit a pastry bag with a small round decorating tip. Turn down the top third of the bag, and fill it with a color that contrasts with the icing on the cookies. Raise the top of the bag and turn in the side. Fold over the top and roll it down to force the icing through the tip. Pipe parallel horizontal stripes across the cookies every $1/2$ inch. Store the pastry bag in a tall glass with a piece of wet paper towel in the bottom, which will prevent the icing from drying out. Take a skewer and pull it through the icing from the top to the bottom of the cookies at 1-inch intervals. Next, pull the skewer from bottom to top of the cookies between the original drag lines to give the marbleized design (1). For a different design, pull the skewer in one direction only through the lines (2). Allow the cookies to dry on a rack. Select another color or colors and repeat these steps in small batches.

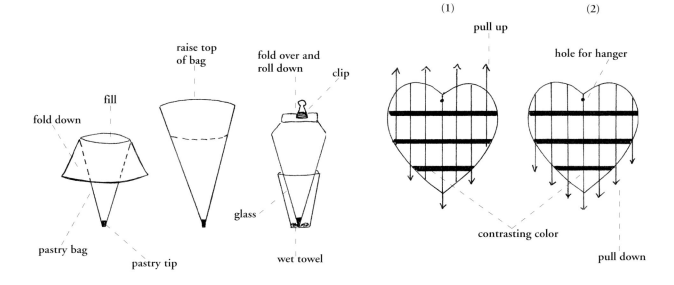

OLD FORMS, NEW WAYS
CANDLESTICK ADAPTERS

Perfect for weddings and other festive occasions, this reusable form, a quick and easy way to embellish a candlestick, candelabra, or other candleholders, can be used in a variety of ways. Here an 8-inch candlestick and a votive holder show two quite different looks. Try using an adapter to hold a flower arrangement in a candlestick without a candle; or place a row of low arrangements in adapters down the center of a table, with or without candles.

154

How to Make an Arrangement Using a Candlestick Adapter

Supplies and materials needed: Green plastic candlestick adapter with a floral foam insert, floral preservative, candleholder insert, candlestick or votive holder, conditioned plant materials (see page 206), candle, and funnel.

To create an arrangement in a candlestick, soak the foam in floral preservative and place it in the adapter and then place the adapter in a candlestick.

Add the candleholder insert. Conceal the adapter by inserting pieces of foliage around the base, such as new growth hemlock and boxwood. Add foliage such as variegated pittosporum with the stems cut short arranged loosely around the form. Finish the arrangement with an assortment of flowers such as white tulips, Queen Anne's lace, tiny bellflowers, candytuft, and green seed pods from native columbine. Be careful to position the flowers so they are loosely arranged and form a graceful arch away from the candlestick. Insert a candle in the holder.

To create an arrangement in a votive holder, place the adapter in the holder and conceal it with short-stemmed foliage including boxwood and galax leaves. Insert blossoms such as tulips with their stems cut short into the foam to form a compact arrangement of colorful flowers. **Note:** Water the arrangements through a small funnel inserted into the top of the foam.

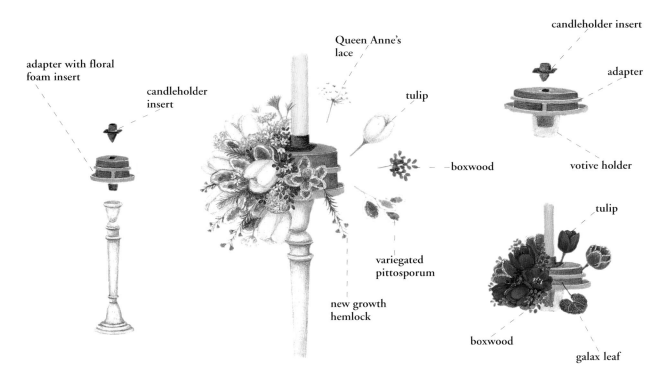

adapter with floral foam insert

candleholder insert

Queen Anne's lace

tulip

boxwood

variegated pittosporum

new growth hemlock

candleholder insert

adapter

votive holder

tulip

boxwood

galax leaf

In the fall, greens and yellows are combined using clusters of bright green nandina berries not yet ripe, yellow roses, bupleurum, variegated acuba, Alexandrian laurel, and sprigs of boxwood and nandina foliage.

During the December holidays, winter gardens provide berries and a profusion of greenery. Here, sprigs of cedar and boxwood arch gracefully from a base of red nandina berries, variegated osmanthus, Burford holly, and hemlock cones.

This ornate candlestick on a delicate lace cloth contains tendrils of variegated ivy and foliage from star anise and nandina plants. Dramatic stargazer lilies and white ranunculus add fragrance.

WEDDING IDEAS

BRIDAL LUNCHEON AND SHOWER

The bride and her attendants, always busy as bees, will appreciate this table setting. A decorative beeskep or straw dome, encircled with bees, is placed in the center of a ring of solidago, asters, safflower, mums, daisies, and other flowers that fill the fields in late summer. These same field flowers are placed in floral foam around the bases of the candlesticks. The desserts are meringue hives filled with delicious honey lemon cream and licorice bees whose wings are toasted almond slices and antennae are saffron threads. Recipes for the meringue hives, filling, and bees follow.

A large dessert basket is filled with meringue hives and marzipan licorice bees. Embroidered bees decorate the napkins while a giant bee finger puppet surveys the contents of the basket.

MERINGUES
6 hives

4 large egg whites, at room temperature
salt
1/2 teaspoon cream of tartar
1 cup sugar

Preheat the oven to 200°F. and place a rack in the lower third of the oven. Cut a sheet of parchment paper to fit a baking sheet. Draw circles for seven sets each of six rings measuring 31/2 inches, 31/4 inches, 23/4 inches, 21/4 inches, 13/4 inches, and 11/4 inches, leaving 1/4 inch between each circle. Beat the egg whites with an electric mixer in a large bowl with a pinch of salt until frothy. Add the cream of tartar. Gradually add the sugar and beat until stiff peaks are formed. Fold back the top third of a 14-inch pastry bag fitted with a round decorating tip with a 1/2-inch opening and spoon in as much meringue as it will hold. Pull up the edges of the bag, folding the top in, and roll it down until the meringue starts to come out of the tip. Holding the bag securely, pipe wide, thin rings of meringue inside the lines drawn on the

parchment paper for all the rings except for the 11/4-inch ones. Hold the bag on the baking sheet at a slight upward angle so the tops of the rings are uniform. After you finish piping these rings, smooth their tops with an offset spatula so they will fit together when stacked. Next fill the 11/4-inch rings with meringue so they form solid circles to use as tops for the hives. Bake the rings for approximately 11/2 hours at 175°F. If you notice the meringues becoming slightly ivory colored, turn off the oven. After turning off the heat, leave the meringues in the oven for several hours or overnight. When removing the rings from the parchment, carefully bend and peel the paper away from the meringues. You can store them in a container in layers of waxed paper until you are ready to use them. **Note:** It is a good idea to make an extra set of rings, although they can be mended with icing.

Marzipan bees clamber over the Johnny-jump-ups and strips of lemon zest to the top of the hive.

MERINGUE HIVES

meringues (see page 161)
icing (see page 153)
lemon honey cream
lemon zest
Johnny jump-ups or other edible flowers
marzipan licorice bees *(opposite)*

Start with the largest ring and gently spread icing on its top surface. Immediately place the next smallest ring on top of the larger ring and ice its top surface. Repeat this step, ending with the top round. After you have assembled the hive, place it on a rack to dry. To fill a hive, invert it and gently spoon the lemon honey cream into the cavity. Turn the hive back over onto the plate. Grate lemon zest over it. Place a spoonful of icing on each side of the hive at the base and a small amount at the front. Insert fresh Johnny-jump-ups or other edible flowers into the icing, with the smallest flowers in the front. Place some icing on the undersides of the bees and gently attach them to the hive. **Note:** Assemble the desserts just before serving them.

LEMON HONEY CREAM

3 eggs, separated
1/2 cup honey
1/2 teaspoon vanilla
1/2 teaspoon gelatin
1/4 cup lemon juice, chilled
1 cup whipping cream
salt

Beat the egg yolks, and then combine them with the honey in the top of a double boiler. Stir the honey mixture constantly until it makes a custard that coats a spoon. Remove the honey mixture from the heat and transfer it to a mixing bowl. Add the vanilla, and set aside. Sprinkle the gelatin over the surface of the lemon juice and stir with a fork. Place the mixture in the top of the double boiler and whisk over low heat until the gelatin dissolves. Stir the gelatin into the honey mixture. Place the bowl in a larger bowl of ice. Stir the mixture until it thickens and cools. Whip the cream with a pinch of salt and fold it into the honey mixture. Refrigerate the lemon honey cream for several hours. **Note:** This recipe makes a soft mixture that can easily be used to fill the meringues. If a slightly stiffer mixture is desired, as for a mousse, increase the gelatin to 1 teaspoon.

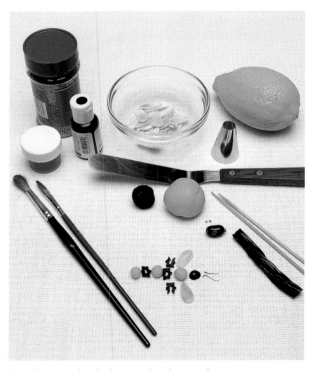

Supplies to make the bees are lined up ready to use.

How to Make Marzipan Licorice Bees

You can make these bees using the rounded ends of black jelly beans for the head and slices of a licorice stick for the black stripes. You can also use black marzipan. Either can be combined with yellow marzipan bodies. Very thin slices of the ridged licorice sticks make realistic legs for the bees.

Supplies and materials needed: Small sharp knife, 7-ounce roll of prepared marzipan, short wooden skewers, lemon-yellow food coloring paste, black food coloring paste (optional), confectioners' sugar, icing (see page 153), licorice jelly beans, 4 x ¹/₂ inch licorice ridged twizzle sticks, lightly toasted sliced almonds, toothpicks, mustard seeds, and saffron threads.

Cut a 1-inch section from the roll of marzipan and store the rest in a small plastic bag. Knead the marzipan until soft and form it into a ball. Make a hole in the center with a skewer. Dip the tip of a skewer into the lemon-yellow paste and put this small amount into the indentation. Dust a cutting board with confectioners' sugar and knead the yellow into the marzipan until it is evenly mixed. Add more color if needed. If the color is too intense a yellow, add more marzipan. When it is well mixed, wrap the marzipan tightly in plastic wrap and store it in an airtight container until you are ready to use it. If you are using marzipan for the face and black stripes, mix another 1-inch section

of marzipan with the black paste.

Use the icing to glue the various pieces of the bee together.

To make each bee, follow these steps.

Head: Cut one-fourth off the end of a black jelly bean or a piece less than ¹/₄-inch round from the black marzipan to form the face.

Body: Cut two ¹/₈-inch-wide slices from the licorice stick or the black marzipan for the black parts of the body. Cut two ¹/₁₆-inch-thick slices from the licorice, with a notch removed, for the legs. Form three balls of yellow marzipan less than ¹/₄ inch in diameter and press two into flat disks about ¹/₈-inch thick for the yellow parts of the body. Shape the third into a pointed piece for the tail. Paint the cut side of the jelly bean or black marzipan head with icing and bond it to one of the yellow disks reserved for the body. Apply more icing to the other side of this disk, and bond it to a ¹/₈-inch slice of licorice or black marzipan. Bond the licorice or black marzipan to the second iced yellow disk, then bond this disk to the other ¹/₈-inch iced licorice or black marzipan slice. Ice the yellow tail section and bond it to the body. With icing, glue the trimmed ¹/₁₆-inch licorice slices underneath the body to use as feet.

Wings: Select two similarly shaped almond slices and gently push them into the body with a dab of icing to form the wings.

Eyes and Antennae: Use a toothpick to put two dots of icing on the face. Put two mustard seeds in the icing for eyes. Select two threads of saffron and attach them as antennae to the head. Transfer the bee to waxed paper to dry.

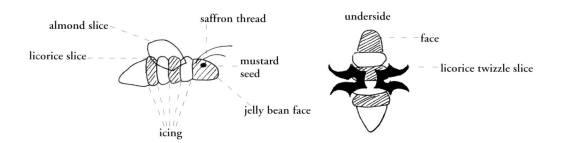

almond slice — saffron thread

licorice slice — mustard seed

jelly bean face

icing

underside

face

licorice twizzle slice

REHEARSAL DINNER

For dinner after the wedding rehearsal, the table is set with a blue runner, a large arrangement of artichokes tinged with purple, yellow, and red Rumba roses, variegated holly, Leyland cypress, Burford holly with green berries, boxwood, variegated aucuba, and Colonial Williamsburg's Imperial Blue dinnerware. Favors at each place greet the guests: a tiny gold silk keepsake pouch for each lady and pieces of gold for each gentleman. For the first course, a small rose of Boston lettuce is filled with fresh Virginia lump crabmeat on an artichoke bottom.

VIRGINIA CRABMEAT ON ARTICHOKE BOTTOMS

4 servings

1/2 pound fresh lump crabmeat
1 1/2 tablespoons plus 2 teaspoons lemon juice

Boston lettuce leaves
1 can (14 ounces) artichoke bottoms
4 tablespoons mayonnaise
1/4 teaspoon dried thyme
lemon zest
4 sprigs parsley
4 sprigs fresh lemon thyme

Pick over the crabmeat and discard any bits of shell or cartilage. Sprinkle 1 1/2 tablespoons of lemon juice over the crabmeat and mix gently to avoid breaking the lumps. Make four roses from the lettuce by taking three or four inner leaves for each one and form them into a circle. Place an artichoke bottom in the center of each rose, then divide the crabmeat into four servings and form a mound on each of the artichokes. Mix 1 to 2 teaspoons lemon juice with the mayonnaise and dried thyme and place a dollop on each serving. Garnish with curled lemon zest and a sprig of parsley and lemon thyme.

How to Make a Keepsake Pouch

Supplies and materials needed: Fine pins, two 10-inch circles of silk or other special fabric, one for the outside and one for the lining, needle and thread to match the outer fabric, fine gold cord, scissors, and large tapestry needle.

Pin the two circles together with the right sides facing inside and sew a 1/4-inch seam around the outside of the circle, leaving a 1 1/2-inch opening. Remove the pins and turn, then press. Slip stitch the opening to close.

Pin around the circle to stabilize the two layers to be sewn together. To form the channel, measure 3/4 inch in from the outer edge and sew a seam around the whole circle. Next measure 3/4 inch inside of this circle and sew a second seam to complete the channel.

Cut two 28-inch pieces of cord. Thread a tapestry needle with one cord. Insert the cord into the channel and come out through the hole you entered. Tie a knot at the end. Repeat this process starting on the opposite side. Tie these two ends together. Pull to tighten.

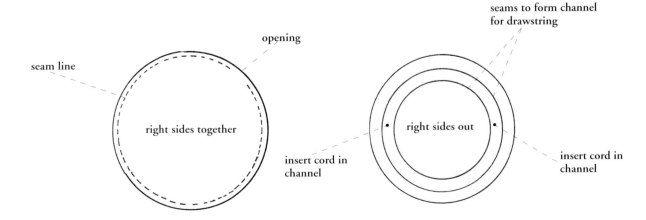

seam line

opening

right sides together

seams to form channel for drawstring

right sides out

insert cord in channel

insert cord in channel

How to Embellish a Guest Book

Supplies and materials needed: Album, pressed flowers, ferns, and leaves (see page 67), label, 1-inch-wide bristle paint brush, white glue, and 2-ply white facial tissue.

Select an album to use as a guest book for the wedding with a plain cover of uncoated paper or one made with art paper in which small pieces of plant material have been embedded.

Choose plant materials such as pressed flowers, ferns, and leaves and position them on the front cover, forming an attractive pattern. Allow space for a label if you are using one. Sketch your design on a separate piece of paper and then remove the pressed plant materials from the cover. Using a coarse bristle brush, spread white glue thinned with water over the surface of the album. Refer to your sketch and carefully place the plant materials on the glue-covered surface, patting them down into the glue.

Take several pieces of 2-ply facial tissue and separate the two plies of each sheet. Tear the edges to feather them. Spread another coat of thinned glue over the whole cover and place the pieces of torn tissue over the dampened cover. Add another layer of glue, and then apply another layer of tissue. Seal the cover with more glue. Allow to dry.

Glue the paper label onto the cover. **Note:** You can embellish album covers as well as those on an address book, a diary, or a notebook with pressed flowers, leaves, and ferns by following these directions.

WEDDING BREAKFAST

Brightly dawns the wedding day. The guests greet the glorious morning with mimosas, freshly baked croissants, and a selection of preserves. At the special request of the bride, her grandmother has brought homemade raspberry jam made from the luscious berries planted by her grandfather and fig-sesame jam from a special friend. The yellow sunflowers, lemons, lantana, and daisies on the table echo the sunshine on this happy day.

MIMOSAS
4 servings

1 cup fresh orange juice
1 bottle chilled champagne
2 tablespoons Grand Marnier
4 mint leaves

Pour ¹/4 cup juice into a champagne glass and slowly add champagne. Top it off with ¹/2 tablespoon Grand Marnier and garnish with a mint leaf.

NANA'S RASPBERRY JAM
7 cups

5 cups raspberries
6 cups sugar
¹/2 teaspoon butter
12-inch spray of lemon verbena
1 envelope (3 fluid ounces) pectin

Sterilize jars and covers to hold 7 cups of jam. Wash and drain the berries, then slightly crush them and stir in the sugar. Pour the berries into an 8-quart saucepan. Add the butter to reduce the foam that is formed during cooking. Add the lemon verbena and bring the berries to a full rolling boil, stirring constantly. Quickly stir in the pectin and return the mixture to a full rolling boil. Boil exactly 1 minute, stirring constantly. Remove from the heat and skim off any foam. Remove the lemon verbena. Fill the jars to within ¹/8 inch from the top, wiping the jar rims if necessary. Put on the lids and screw on the metal bands. Turn the jars upside down for 5 minutes, then upright them and leave at room temperature for 24 hours.

FIG-SESAME JAM
3¹/2 cups

Although figs were commonly grown in colonial Virginia, they were not universally beloved. Philip Vickers Fithian, who tutored Robert Carter's children at Nomini Hall plantation, noted in his diary on August 26, 1774: "We gathered some Figs, the Ladies seem fond of them, I cannot endure them." Had he tasted this jam, he might have changed his mind.

2 pounds fresh figs
1¹/4 cups sugar
³/4 cup water
1 tablespoon lemon zest
2 tablespoons lemon juice
¹/4 cup sesame seeds

Sterilize enough jars and seals to hold 3¹/2 cups of jam. Trim and quarter the figs, which should be firm and ripe. Simmer the sugar and water over low heat in a large, heavy saucepan until the sugar is dissolved, stirring constantly. Gently stir in the figs, lemon zest, and lemon juice. Simmer over low heat, uncovered, about 1³/4 to 2 hours, or until thick and syrupy, stirring occasionally. While the jam is cooking, put the sesame seeds in a small pan over medium heat and stir them until they brown. Remove them from the heat. When the jam has finished cooking, gently stir in the sesame seeds. Pour the jam into the jars and seal them.

SUMMER WEDDINGS

Ever since that famous couple started their life together in the Garden of Eden, many brides and grooms have held their weddings in a variety of outdoor settings. Now that modern technology has made possible tents that are self-contained centers for entertaining, even the threat of inclement weather is not a worry.

A plantation overlooking the James River is an idyllic setting for a late summer wedding. The cool blue and white colors of the decorations are welcome in the heat of a Tidewater August. Guests have an impressive view of the James River from the large, white reception tent. French blue tablecloths and white chairs, and blue delphiniums, white lilies, larkspur, hydrangeas, phlox, gladiolas, and echinops in dramatic sprays on the tent poles and in the table decorations repeat the colors of the flowers carried by the wedding party.

Above: The flowers used here are white gladiolas, lilies, phlox, blue delphiniums, and echinops.

Left: A centerpiece of varying shades of blue hydrangeas, Montecasino asters, larkspur, delphiniums, echinops, field grasses, and large Maaike roses with pale pink centers makes a stunning statement on the French blue tablecloth.

The bride's bouquet of blue hydrangeas and fully opened Maaike roses is tied with a satin ribbon.

How to Use Floral Foam Cages to Decorate in the Round

Supplies and materials needed: Three 7 x 4¹/₂ x 3¹/₄ inch cages filled with floral foam for each tent pole, #22 gauge green floral wire, duct tape, green floral adhesive tape, and conditioned plant materials (see page 206).

Soak the cages filled with floral foam blocks in water overnight or until saturated. Run floral wire through the first cage and tightly fasten it in the back so it will not open. Use duct tape to secure the top tab on the cage to the pole. With the handle pointing downward, use more duct tape to secure the handle to the pole. Wrap floral tape around the cage and pole. Repeat with the other cages on the pole. If the reception is to be held in a small tent, two cages secured to opposite sides of the pole would be sufficient.

Insert pieces of green foliage at the back of the forms. Select flowers that will radiate out from the top, such as these dramatic spikes of white gladiolas, and place them in front of the foliage. Finally, add flowers that will accent the arrangement, such as white lilies, blue hydrangeas, white phlox, and purple echinops. Be sure your design is well balanced with a mixture of colors and textures.

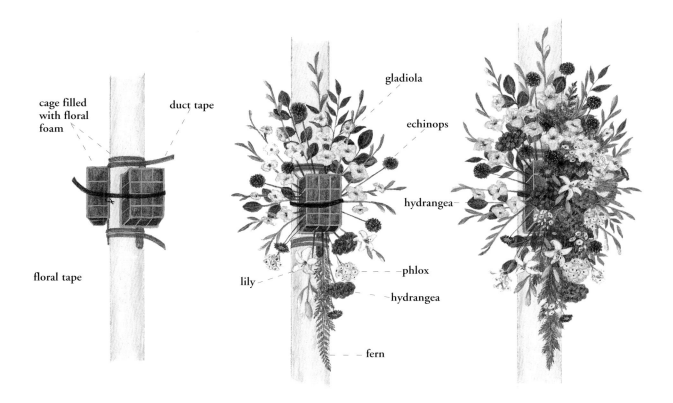

cage filled with floral foam

duct tape

floral tape

gladiola

echinops

hydrangea

lily

phlox

hydrangea

fern

Clockwise from the left: The flower girl's basket, her floral headband, and a nosegay, or tussie-mussie, in a silver holder carried by a bridesmaid all feature blue delphiniums and baby's breath.

How to Make a Headband for the Flower Girl

Supplies and materials needed: Coat hanger wire or other heavy wire, floral tape, #28 gauge spool wire, conditioned plant materials such as delphiniums and baby's breath (see page 206), and plant mister.

Measure the size of the flower girl's head and cut a piece of heavy wire to fit loosely, allowing for extra wire to form interlocking loops. Cover the wire with the tape. Attach the end of the spool wire to the wire band. Leaving the wire attached to the spool, hold a few sprigs of delphiniums and baby's breath on the headband and wrap the stem ends to the frame with the wire. Be careful to cover the ends of the previous pieces as you go. Continue to add the flowers until you have covered the headband. Tuck the final bunch under the flowers of the first bunch. Mist the headband well and refrigerate it in a plastic bag until the flower girl is ready to wear it.

How to Make a Basket for the Flower Girl

Supplies and materials needed: Plastic liner, small, white basket, block of instant deluxe floral foam, conditioned plant materials (see page 206), and ribbon.

Find a plastic container such as a yogurt cup to use as a liner that fits into the basket. Cut a piece of floral foam to fit into the liner and soak it in water. Place the floral foam inside the liner and the liner into the basket. Arrange the flowers to keep them below the handle so the flower girl can carry the basket easily. You can arrange the flowers to appear to spill out of the basket on the sides. The center contains more of the same flowers, roses, and stock. After filling the basket, tie a bow around a base of the handle.

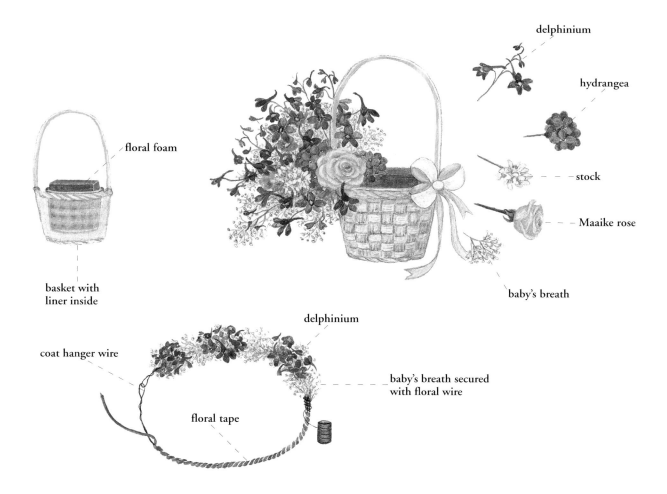

floral foam

basket with liner inside

delphinium

hydrangea

stock

Maaike rose

baby's breath

coat hanger wire

delphinium

baby's breath secured with floral wire

floral tape

A Winter Wedding Reception at the Williamsburg Inn

Indoor winter weddings, too, can reflect nature. The East Lounge of the Williamsburg Inn is transformed into a snowy winter wonderland to create an elegant setting for a December wedding reception. Christmas trees of different heights are arranged in a semicircle on either side of the fireplace. Tiny clear lights glow on all the trees. White poinsettia blossoms and gilded privet rest on the branches, giving the impression of trees covered with glistening snow. Winter greens and white flowers are used throughout, including the flowers for the wedding party. A gilded angel on a large wreath of fresh noble fir hangs above the mantel.

Poinsettia branches were cut from plants and immediately held in a flame to sear the stems and then placed in pails of water until needed. Treated in this manner, they will remain fresh for one or two days. The poinsettias are positioned on the branches to face outward. Pieces of fresh privet, about twelve inches long, are sprayed with a shiny gold floral paint. Placed deep within the branches, they reflect and intensify the lights, also placed deep within the trees.

Tiers of the large, white wedding cake are iced with green foliage and white lilies of the valley. A romantic pastillage gazebo, a tiny replica of the one in the Nelson-Galt House garden, is placed on top. Fresh lily of the valley, white heather, maidenhair fern, and camellia foliage encircle the base of the cake.

Above: An assortment of finger foods is offered on a large table centered with an arrangement of cut amaryllis, maidenhair fern, white pine, narcissus, white roses, and white heather.

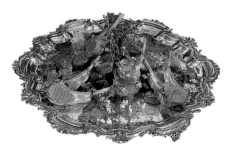

The groom's cake, a Yule log, or bûche de Nöel, is placed in front of the fire on a tartan cloth. This large log, covered with rich chocolate bark, is placed on a silver platter surrounded by meringue mushrooms dusted with cocoa powder. Sprigs of maidenhair ferns and white heather are tucked around the mushrooms.

YULE LOG

$^1/_2$ cup plus 1 teaspoon cake flour
6 egg yolks
$6^1/_2$ tablespoons sugar, divided
4 egg whites

Preheat the oven to 400°F. Grease well the bottom and sides of a 15 x 10$^1/_2$ x 1 inch jelly roll pan. Line the bottom with waxed paper and grease and flour it. Sift the flour after measuring. Beat the egg yolks and 2 tablespoons sugar until fluffy and set aside. Whip the egg whites with the remaining sugar until soft peaks form. Alternate folding the egg whites and flour into the egg yolks, ending with the egg whites. Spread the mixture in the pan and bake at 400°F. about 10 minutes until the cake is a light golden color. Turn the cake out on a damp tea towel covered with waxed paper. Starting at the long edge, roll the towel, waxed paper, and cake into a tight roll and let it cool. Carefully unroll the cake and spread the exposed side with buttercream icing. Do not spread the icing to the edge of the cake. Leave a $^1/_2$-inch border free of icing. Roll up the cake again, removing the towel and waxed paper. Place it seam side down and refrigerate. After it is chilled, cut a piece on the diagonal from one end of the roll. Cut a different-sized piece on the diagonal from the other end. Coat the noncut ends of the pieces with buttercream icing and attach them to the log to resemble limbs. Spread the remaining buttercream icing on the cake. Use a spatula, cake comb, or fish scaler to give it the texture of a log. Place chocolate bark on the log while the icing is still sticky, then transfer it to a bed of greenery surrounded by meringue mushrooms.

BUTTERCREAM ICING

6 ounces unsweetened chocolate
1 3/4 cups unsalted butter, room temperature
3 cups confectioners' sugar
2 tablespoons water

Melt the chocolate in the top of a double boiler over simmering, not boiling, water. Remove the chocolate from the heat, and let it cool. Whip the butter and sugar until fluffy. Slowly add the water, then the chocolate, to the butter mixture.

CHOCOLATE BARK

1/2 pound semisweet chocolate

Melt the chocolate in the top of a double boiler over simmering, not boiling, water until smooth. Pour the chocolate on two cookie sheets. Smooth the chocolate with a metal spatula to form a layer about 1/16-inch thick. Use as few strokes as possible so the chocolate will not become overworked and brittle as it chills. Refrigerate the chocolate until it is dry and cold. Remove the trays from the refrigerator and let the chocolate soften slightly. Using the metal spatula, remove the chocolate in curls, strips, or fragments. Refrigerate these pieces until they harden. Store the pieces in an airtight container until you are ready to use them.

MERINGUE MUSHROOMS

2 large egg whites, room temperature
1/4 teaspoon cream of tartar
1/2 cup sugar
2 ounces semisweet chocolate

Preheat the oven to 200°F. Line two cookie sheets with parchment paper. In the small bowl of an electric mixer, beat the egg whites and cream of tartar on low until foamy. Continue to beat on high, adding sugar gradually until stiff and glossy peaks form. Spoon the meringue into a pastry bag (see page 153) fitted with a 1/2-inch plain tip. On the first cookie sheet, pipe fifteen to twenty 3/4- to 1 1/2-inch domed rounds. Wet your finger with water and smooth the tops. On the second cookie sheet, pipe the same number of 1- to 1 1/2-inch peaked mounds for the stems. Bake the meringues until they are dry and beginning to color, about 1 3/4 hours. The caps will take longer to dry than the stems. Let them cool completely and remove from the parchment. Melt the chocolate in the top of a double boiler over simmering, not boiling, water. Remove the chocolate from the heat and let it cool. Scoop out a small amount of crisp meringue from the centers of the flat sides of the caps. Spoon melted chocolate into each hole and immediately put the tip of the stems into the chocolate. Place some of the caps at a slight angle to add interest. Allow to dry. Store the mushrooms in an airtight container until ready to use. Dust the mushrooms with cocoa powder before using them.

To carry out the green and white theme, white amaryllis dominate this dramatic arrangement on a dark green cloth. Long branches of white heather fan out over the cloth and paper-white narcissus and white ranunculus complete the design.

The bride's bouquet rests on an heirloom hand-embroidered lace cloth, its colors the greens and whites of winter. White pine from a snowy garden is combined with a variety of elegant flowers, herbs, and foliage. In the background, a silver urn holds white roses, ranunculus, and maidenhair fern accented with white talo berries.

Supplies and materials needed: Plastic floral bouquet holder with handle fitted with floral foam, floral preservative, clippers, and conditioned plant materials (see page 206).

Soak the holder until well saturated in floral preservative. Insert sprigs of white pine, camellia leaves, variegated moonshadow euonymus, and maidenhair fern around the edge of the form. Next, take the flowers with the largest blooms, such as white ranunculus and spray roses, and place them randomly at the center to stand out against the green foliage. Add the smaller pieces of white heather, rosemary sprigs, lilies of the valley, and paper-white narcissus for fragrance and contrasting textures. Use these flowers to fill open spaces at different heights to give the bouquet a graceful dimension. The white pine and euonymus lend an elegant and tapering line to the cascade when held by the bride.

How to Make a Bridal Bouquet

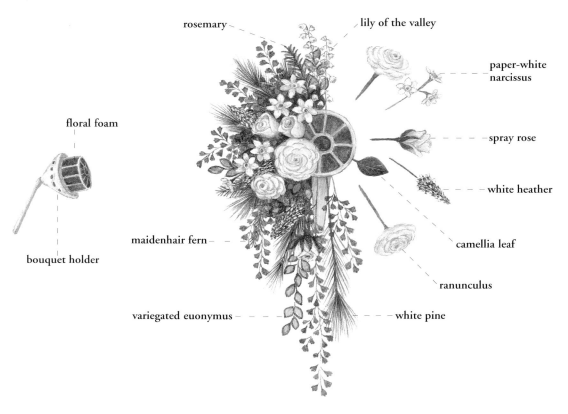

rosemary

lily of the valley

paper-white narcissus

floral foam

spray rose

white heather

camellia leaf

maidenhair fern

ranunculus

bouquet holder

variegated euonymus

white pine

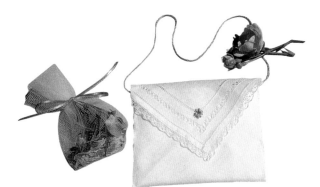

Make a small design on the flap with the blue embroidery thread and sew on the ribbon with a safety pin to attach the sachet inside the bride's gown. Fill the netting with herbs, tie it with a piece of tiny blue ribbon, and insert the herbs into the sachet. **Note:** After the wedding, the bride can easily unstitch the handkerchief and use it for special occasions.

How to Make a Wedding Sachet

Much has been written about the language of flowers and the symbolism of herbs. One family has a tradition of loaning a bride a tiny, embroidered linen bag filled with a sachet of "wedding herbs"—rose petals, rosemary, violets, lavender, sage, and an ivy leaf—to pin inside her wedding dress. Worn by several generations of brides, this borrowed item ensures good luck and a long life to the bride and the groom.

To start a new tradition, fill a beautiful handkerchief with a net bag of fresh or dried herbs, tied with a blue ribbon, and present the sachet to the bride.

Supplies and materials needed: Handkerchief, needle, thread, scissors, blue embroidery thread, blue ribbon, 6-inch circle of net, and dried "wedding herbs."

With the prettiest or most ornate corner of a new or heirloom 8 x 8 inch handkerchief at the upper right (corner F), measure about 2 1/2 inches from corners F and C. Fold the handkerchief at fold line A, then fold back corner A. Next fold the handkerchief at fold line B, then fold back corner B. Fold the rectangle at fold line C, then fold up to fold line D, then to fold line E. Corner F will be a pretty flap for the bag when turned down. Close the sides of the sachet with tiny stitches of matching thread on the back.

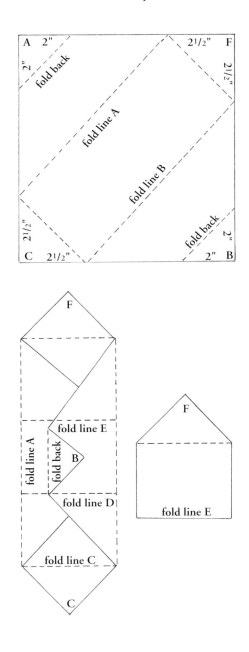

GIFT IDEAS

GIFTS FROM THE GARDEN

Colonial Williamsburg's gardens are a rich source of ideas for decorative and useful gifts that will give lasting pleasure to those who receive them. You can use spices and herbs, especially the ever-popular lavender, to make a variety of gifts including pomanders, potpourri, sachets, and even Christmas ornaments.

A love of nature in the eighteenth century influenced many areas of the arts. Textiles, ceramics, silver, furniture designs, prints, paintings, and accessories incorporating botanical subjects were particularly popular. Colonial Williamsburg offers reproductions of some from its collection based on original documents. Select a print or a piece of wallpaper to decoupage a watering can or to cover and line a bandbox.

A gift any gardener can put to use immediately is a pot you have painted with a "faux" lead finish or a trough or planter fabricated from cement that look like the old stones ones so coveted today. Take the ideas that follow and create special remembrances to give your family and friends.

POMANDERS AND POTPOURRI

Somehow, Christmas would not be the same without making pomanders from oranges, clementines, limes, lemons, kumquats, limequats, or even apples. Their spicy fragrance evokes the winter holidays and all its festivities.

Part of the pleasure of potpourri comes from making it. Try some recipes to familiarize yourself with different combinations of plant materials and scents as they did in colonial times. Add herbs from a friend's garden or flowers from a memorable event to remind you of your many gifts from the garden.

How to Make a Pomander

Supplies and materials needed: Thin-skinned fruit, long-stemmed cloves, skewers or strong toothpicks, 1/4 cup ground cinnamon, 1/4 cup cloves, 1/4 cup nutmeg, 1/4 cup allspice, 1/4 cup ginger, 1/4 cup powdered orrisroot, ribbon, and soft pencil.

To make a pomander that will last for months, you will need to cover the fruit totally with cloves. To make the job easier, use skewers or toothpicks to make

holes and then insert the cloves. The holes should be evenly spaced 1/8 inch apart. Completely cover with cloves. Combine the cinnamon, cloves, nutmeg, allspice, ginger, and orrisroot in a shallow bowl. Place the pomander in the bowl and roll the fruit in the spices and orrisroot until it is completely covered. Rotate it frequently. It will shrink and harden as it dries. Once dry, tie the pomander with a ribbon.

To decorate fruit with clove designs, draw the patterns lightly on the fruit with a soft pencil. Make holes with a skewer. Vary the designs.

How to Make Potpourri

The 1758 edition of *The Compleat Housewife; or, Accomplish'd Gentlewoman's COMPANION* includes this potpourri recipe: "Take of orrice roots, sweet calamus, cypress roots, of dried lemon-peel, and dried orange-peel; of each a pound; a peck of dried roses; make all these into a gross powder; coriander seed four ounces, nutmegs an ounce and a half, an ounce of cloves; make all these into fine powder and mix with the other; add musk and ambergrease; then take four large handfuls of lavender-flowers dried and rubb'd; mix all together, with some bits of cotton perfumed with essences, and put it up into silk bags to lay with your linen."

There are many modern recipes for potpourri but here is one by George Gross, a Virginia chemist and herbalist who gladly shared his wealth of knowledge and experience. He advised to "sniff sharply in short stints, but remember violet and orris desensitize the nose. Use care in adding strongly odorous materials, some disappear forever while others come back with a vengeance. Remember that natural products vary widely according to the source, season, and state of growth. Powdered ingredients are the most effective. Store all aromatics in glass containers. Mixes require aging to blend so allow three to five days to get a good idea of the mixture. The final scent will take thirty days."

Supplies and materials needed: Four glass jars with lids, *Base:* 1¹/₂ cups dried rose petals, ³/₈ cup dried lavender flowers, ¹/₄ cup sandalwood chips, *Modifier:* 1 teaspoon powdered cloves, ¹/₂ teaspoon ground cinnamon, ¹/₂ teaspoon powdered allspice, ¹/₂ teaspoon powdered nutmeg, ¹/₂ teaspoon powdered cardamom, *Fixative:* 2 teaspoons powdered orrisroot, 2 teaspoons coarsely chopped calamus root, 2¹/₂ teaspoons dried chopped patchouli leaves, 1 teaspoon powdered vetiver root, ¹/₂ teaspoon powdered tonka bean, *Top Note:* ¹/₄ teaspoon each rose oil, neroli (orange blossom) oil, and jasmine oil.

In a glass jar, mix the base and modifier ingredients and then add the powdered vetiver and tonka bean from the ingredients for the fixative. In three separate glass jars with lids, mix the rose oil with the orrisroot, the jasmine oil with the patchouli leaves, and the neroli oil with the calamus root. Let the oils absorb into the fixatives for at least 3 days, then add them to the dry ingredients, mixing well. Let the potpourri age in the dark for 2 weeks. Mix again. After 4 weeks, it will be properly aged and can be placed in a covered potpourri jar. Uncover the jar to release the fragrance, but keep it covered when not in use. This potpourri will last for many years. **Note:** Always wear gloves when handling the oils.

DECOUPAGE GIFTS

Decoupage accessories in the collections at Colonial Williamsburg reflect the interest during colonial times in new and exotic plants featured in botanical prints, drawings, and paintings. In the eighteenth century, young ladies colored English prints such as those in Robert Sayer's book titled *The Ladies Amusement; or, Whole Art of Japanning Made Easy.* Frequently, the botanical subjects in the prints were cut out with embroidery scissors, glued to the top of a box or other surface, and coated with many layers of varnish to secure and to protect the images. Visitors today to the James Geddy House enjoy watching young ladies in costume practice the art of watercolor painting and examining examples of japanning.

Present-day decoupage is much the same process as in earlier times. Artists use this craft in many new ways, employing a variety of papers and fabrics. Today's artists are encouraged to make photocopies so no originals are used. Antique examples of flat decoupage and the lesser-known three-dimensional decoupage have inspired these modern accessories.

How to Decoupage a Watering Can

Supplies and materials needed: Metal watering can, mineral spirits, four 1-inch-wide paint brushes, metal primer, #400 sandpaper, paint, tack cloth, laser prints or paper motifs, fine, sharp manicure scissors or iris scissors, tweezers, sheet of glass or plastic, white glue, waxed paper, roller or brayer, cloth, and nonyellowing satin varnish compatible with the paint.

Clean the watering can with mineral spirits, dry thoroughly, and brush on two or three coats of primer to cover the can. Use a primer compatible with the type of material from which the can is made. Galvanized metals, for example, take a specific kind of primer. Lightly sand the can, then apply a coat of paint, and lightly sand it again after the paint has dried thoroughly. Apply a second coat of paint, sanding the can after it dries. Remove any surface dust with the tack cloth.

Select a print or paper motif to use (you can also use trims, pressed flowers, or other suitable objects). Combine several images to create a composite image. Cut away the outside outline, leaving the most delicate areas until last. Bring the scissors up from beneath the print and carefully cut away any inner areas. Using tweezers, place the cut images onto the can to position them, marking lightly with a pencil for reference. Remove the images and place them face down on a sheet of glass or a flat plastic surface. Take a soft brush and coat the back surface of the first image thoroughly with thinned white glue. Carefully place the glued side on the painted surface according to the reference marks. Place a sheet of waxed paper on top of the image and flatten, with the roller or brayer, removing any air pockets and excess glue with a slightly dampened cloth. Allow the surface to dry. Repeat with the other images, trims, dried flowers, or other objects.

Use a good-quality brush to apply several coats of varnish to the watering can's surface. Allow it to dry thoroughly between coats. After you have applied three or four coats, sand the can lightly with fine sandpaper. The surface should be smooth and the applied decorations well covered by the varnish. The metal vase pictured with the watering can was decoupaged in the same way. **Note:** Some surfaces will require up to thirty coats of varnish, but four to six coats will be sufficient for a piece that will not receive much wear.

You can also decoupage glass objects, including

glass plates, bowls, hurricane shades—sometimes made into lamp bases—and wooden accessories. Before applying decorations to glass, wash and dry the glass thoroughly. If you decoupage a hurricane shade or globe, glue the images to the inside of the glass. Be careful to eliminate all air pockets. Apply paint over the back of the glued image or images and remaining clear glass areas to form the background.

The iris prints on the glass plate (see page 193) were glued to the underside of the plate; then decorative papers for the border were applied on top of the iris. The separate sections of the decorative border were outlined with gold paint. The back of the plate was then given a coat of paint and when dry, a coat of varnish was added to give it a durable finish.

How to Create a Three-Dimensional Decoupage for a Tray

Mark Catesby, the English naturalist who came to Virginia in the eighteenth century, painted many native birds, including the cardinal used on the tray *(below right)*. The three-dimensional floral print *(below left)* is framed and ready to hang. It could also be used to decorate a tray. Colonial Williamsburg has several examples of this decorative technique in its collections.

Supplies and material needed: Wooden tray, four 1-inch-wide paint brushes, wood primer, #400 sandpaper, tack cloth, paint, four pieces of $1/2$ x $3/16$ inch wood cut to fit the inside of the tray, four $3/16$-inch-wide pieces of dollhouse molding cut to fit the inside of the tray, nonyellowing satin varnish compatible with the paint, three copies of a print, fine, sharp manicure scissors or iris scissors, tweezers, sheet of plate glass, white glue, waxed paper, roller or brayer, dowel, and a piece of plate glass cut to fit into the tray.

Brush on one coat of primer. After it dries, lightly sand it and remove all dust with the tack cloth. Apply two coats of paint, lightly sanding the tray after each coat has dried. Paint the pieces of wood and the pieces of dollhouse molding. After they have dried, varnish them and the tray.

Have three copies of the same print. Good-quality laser copies are satisfactory. Cut out the whole image from the first copy as you would for a flat decoupage. Position this cutout on the tray with tweezers. Mark lightly with a pencil, then place it face down on a sheet of glass and apply a coat of thinned glue to the entire back surface. Place the image on the tray and cover it with waxed paper. Work out any air bubbles with a roller or brayer.

With the second copy, cut details from the image that you will apply as raised elements on the first copy. Start by cutting out a separate image of the cardinal. Curve it over a dowel. Add drops of glue at the end of the tail, the base of the tail, the lower foot, the neck, the wing tip, and the top of the crest on the head, and then attach it slightly within the first copy of the cardinal so there are raised areas between the glue points.

With the third copy, cut out the cardinal's head, including the shoulder, and curve it over the dowel. Put a drop of glue on the shoulder and attach it on the second copy of the cardinal. Do not glue the top crest. Cut out the wing, curve it over the dowel, put a drop of glue on the shoulder and on the wing tip, and attach it over the second copy of the wing so you

achieve a pronounced curve.

Cut out leaves and separate sections of the nut from the second copy and curve them over the dowel. Apply drops of glue only to the bottom edges and top points of the leaves and only the outside edges of the nut sections. Attach them on top of the first copy. **Note:** If there is shading on a leaf, it should be curled to emphasize it. It is not necessary to cover each leaf. Add only the portions that will contribute to a pleasing composition. A third copy of leaves and nut sections can be used but is not necessary.

Glue the pieces of wood to the bottom and sides of the tray, which will raise the glass above the three-dimensional decoration. Glue the pieces of molding on top of the glass and the sides of the tray. This step will hold the glass in place. **Note:** Do not varnish the print if it is protected by glass.

STONE TROUGHS AND GARDEN POTS

Rustic cement troughs made according to these instructions take on a weathered patina in a short time and resemble the original carved stone troughs or planters from farms and estates that find their way to antique shops. They can be used as planters, birdbaths, or even to chill wine or beer for alfresco entertaining. You can create a convincing "faux" lead finish on any ordinary terra-cotta pot with these directions.

How to Make a "Faux" Stone Trough

Supplies and materials needed: 13 x 9 x 6 inch plastic form without a lip or heavy cardboard box, large heavy-weight trash bags or strong plastic sheeting, masking tape or duct tape, rubber gloves, face mask, 6-cup plastic pitcher, dry peat moss, vermiculite, portland cement, plastic wheelbarrow or large plastic mason's trough, small hoe, trowel, or three-pronged cultivator, 4 x 4 x 2 inch plastic sandwich box, skewers, plant mister, shells (optional), 6 x 12 inch board, 10 x ¹/₂ inch dowel, large wire brush with a long handle, and vinegar.

Assemble all the materials in a garage or other protected or shady area where you plan to leave the form to cure. Cover the exterior of the form completely with trash bags or sheeting and secure the bags or sheeting with tape. Do not worry about any folds and wrinkles in the plastic—they will add texture. Place it on a plastic-covered table or board so you will be able to turn it.

Wear gloves and a mask and have a ready supply of water nearby. Put 4¹/₂ 6-cup pitchers each of peat moss (broken up into small pieces), vermiculite, and portland cement into a wheelbarrow or mason's trough. Mix them thoroughly with a small hoe, trowel, or cultivator and your hands. Gradually moisten the mixture with water until it is the consistency of cottage cheese. If the mixture is too wet, it will slide off the form. Mix it with your hands to break up any lumps. When the mixture can be made into a ball, you are ready for the next step. Add water as needed so the mixture does not dry out.

Turn the form bottom side up. Use the sandwich box to make blocks with the mixture. Starting at the bottom edge of the form, firmly pat a block of the mixture onto the form. If the mixture slides down while you are making the trough, push it up as necessary. If it continues to slide, the mixture is too wet. Wait a few minutes until it is more manageable. Continue making blocks and applying them to the form until the bottom and sides are at least 2 to 3 inches thick. Measure with a bamboo skewer, especially on the corners, to make sure the thickness is uniform. Lightly mist the surface of the form frequently to keep it from cracking. You may press shells or other objects into the wet mixture if you like the look. After the form is coated with the mixture, use the small board to flatten the surface that will be the bottom so the trough will sit evenly. Insert a dowel to add drainage holes in the bottom of the trough. Be sure the dowel goes all the way through the mixture to the form. **Note:** Immediately after the trough is finished, hose off all the equipment used before the mixture hardens.

Cover the trough loosely with the bags or sheeting and leave it in the shade or in a protected area on the plastic-covered board or table. After 24 hours, check to see whether the trough is well set and, if so, carefully turn the trough and remove the form. If any cracks or breaks occur while removing the form, make more of the mixture, thoroughly spray the damaged area with water, and patch the trough with wet mixture. Use the wire brush to rough up the surface, to remove any unwanted overlapping areas, and to soften the edges.

Cure the trough in a well-ventilated area for 4 to 6 weeks, then move it outside so the rain will rinse out the chemicals. Hose off the trough periodically to help the curing process.

Before using the trough, you will need to neu-

tralize the alkalinity. Leave it outside over the fall and winter, or drench the trough with a vinegar-water solution, then rinse it well with water.

To age the trough, once it has dried, wet the outside surface with water and coat it with yogurt, buttermilk, or liquid manure to encourage algae and moss growth. Crumble pieces of moss and pat onto the wet surface.

When using your trough as a planter, be sure the holes you made earlier provide drainage. If not, use a masonry bit to open them. Put pieces of plastic screening over the holes, fill the planter about one-quarter full with gravel, then with potting soil. **Note:** When fabricating such a planter, make four 4-inch patties about 1 1/2 inches tall. You can use these to elevate the planter for more drainage.

These forms can be made in a variety of sizes and shapes. The mottled and porous surface will encourage the growth of moss. All are made by the same method, known as "hypertufa." These troughs can be shaped over old dishpans, cartons, plastic storage units, plastic flower boxes, or you can sculpt them freehand from ingredients available in garden centers and builder's supply stores. Be sure the form you use does not have a lip that would prevent removing the mold. A large form, especially if it is to be used in cold climates, should be reinforced with a commercial mixture of fibers manufactured to strengthen large cast forms (available from concrete suppliers) following

the manufacturer's directions. When the trough is dry, burn off any fibers that protrude.

Shells are pressed into the sides of this trough to give it an interesting look.

How to Apply a "Faux" Lead Finish to a Garden Pot

Supplies and materials needed: Four 1-inch-wide paint brushes, primer sealer for porous materials, unpainted terra-cotta pot, 1 pint dark charcoal gray exterior latex paint with low luster finish, 1 pint pale bluish-green interior latex paint with eggshell finish, soft, lint-free cloths, and nonyellowing latex matte varnish.

Brush one coat of primer sealer on the pot. Allow it to dry. Apply two coats of dark charcoal gray paint, drying thoroughly between coats. Use the pale bluish-green paint as a wash. Slightly dilute 1 cup of this paint with 1/4 cup of water. Because latex paint dries quickly, apply this color to one small section of the pot at a time. Allow the bluish-green wash to seep into the crevices. Partially rub off this wash immediately with the cloth before it dries. Continue this procedure over the entire surface. The rim and the inside should be painted last.

If your container has a raised decoration, highlight it with the gray paint using an almost dry brush. Apply several coats of varnish with a good-quality brush to prevent the paint from flaking if the pots are used outdoors. **Note:** You can use this finish on any terra-cotta container.

BANDBOXES

Bandboxes were fashionable storage accessories in the early nineteenth century in which people kept hats, shirt collars, laces, trinkets, and finery of all sorts. The papers used to cover these boxes were often designed especially for this purpose and called hat papers. You can make your own bandbox or purchase papier-mâché or wooden boxes in a variety of sizes and shapes that are ready to cover from a craft store.

How to Make a Bandbox

Supplies and materials needed: Scissors or craft knife, cutting mat, heavy poster board, bristol board, or other heavy paper, #8 crewel needle, and fine linen thread or 1-inch-wide paper tape.

Follow these instructions to make an oval box 5 x 3³/4 x 3 inches. Cut a 5 x 3³/4 x 3 inch oval from the heavy paper and mark it with a T for the top. Using this oval as a pattern, cut a second one for the bottom, labeling it B. Trim off ¹/16 inch around the circumference of B. Next, make bands for the top and bottom of the box. Cut the two strips so the grain of the paper runs perpendicular to the box rim to enable the strips to bend evenly. Cut a strip 15 x ⁷/8 inches for the narrow band for the top. Cut a strip 15 x 3 inches for the wider band for the bottom. Each strip allows for a 1-inch overlap. You can sew or tape the pieces to assemble the box.

The traditional method is sewing. Make small holes with your needle every ¹/2 inch around the top, putting the holes ¹/8 inch from the edge. Either whip stitch or use a blanket stitch to attach the top to the narrow band and the bottom to the wider band. Be sure the bands are outside but even with the top or

bottom. Stitch in place. Trim each band so the ends overlap ¹/2 inch. Place the top over the bottom, making sure there is room for a decorative covering.

To join the pieces by taping, attach half the width of the tape along one long edge of the narrow band. Cut a V every ¹/3 inch in the unattached edge of the tape, which will ensure that the tape will be flat when folded over the top. Be careful not to cut into the band. Hold the narrow band outside and even with the top, or larger, piece. Fold each tab separately, keeping the folded tabs as flat as possible. It is helpful to put the top over a flat surface such as a jar with a smooth top. Tape the narrow overlapping sections of the band both inside and outside. Repeat with the bottom and the wider band. The top should fit easily over the bottom. If it is too snug, pull the wide side band overlap slightly inward on the top edge and retape this overlap.

Note: To make a larger box, decide on the size and shape of the top and the height of the box. Cut the top and bottom and remove ¹/16 inch around the bottom piece. The narrow and wider bands should measure the circumference of the top plus 1 inch in length for the overlap. Cut the wider band the height of the box.

How to Cover a Bandbox

Supplies and materials needed: Decorative paper for the outer covering, white glue, 1-inch brush, scissors, ruler, brayer, 6-inch section of large dowel, lining paper, and waxed paper.

Trace the top on the wrong side of the decorative paper selected for the exterior. Consider the placement if there is a pattern. Add ¹/2-inch margin around the outside. Trace the narrow band and add ¹/2 inch to the lower edge. Trace the wider band and add ¹/2 inch to both edges. Trace the bottom. Do not increase the size of this piece. Cut out all traced pieces of decorative paper.

Some papers are easier to work with than others. Glue tends to sink into some commercial papier-mâché boxes. If using one of these boxes, put glue on both surfaces, or just on the paper you are using to cover the box. Thin the glue with water until it spreads easily. Spread the glue on the outside of the top. Center the top onto the piece of paper with the extra margin even on all sides. Press out any air bubbles and smooth out the whole area with the brayer or dowel. You can also use your fingers to move any air bubbles to the edge but do it quickly before the glue becomes tacky. Make slits in the paper just up to the edge of the top. Apply glue to these tabs and fold them onto the narrow band. Smooth evenly.

Take the paper for the narrow band, apply glue to all but the extra 1/2 inch, and carefully align the paper at the top edge, with the extra material at the bottom. Cut slits as you did for the top, apply glue, and fold the tabs to the inside.

Apply glue to all but the extra 1/2 inch on both edges to the paper for the wider band. Center the paper on the wider band with the extra margin even on both sides. Carefully wrap the paper around the wider band. Work out any air bubbles with the brayer or your fingers. Make slits on the top edge, apply glue, bend

these tabs to the inside, and smooth carefully. On the bottom, cut Vs around the edge every 1/3 inch, apply glue, fold these tabs onto the base, and smooth carefully. Glue the bottom piece over these tabs to finish the outside.

Many people like to use newspaper for the lining, which is traditional, but you can use any paper. To line the inside of the box, trace the top on the lining paper. Cut out, check the fit, and glue to the inside of the top. Trace the inside of the narrow band on the lining paper, slightly narrower than the outside measurement. Cut and glue in place. For the inside of the wider band, trace a slightly narrower piece than the total width on the lining paper. It can be cut in half for ease of handling. Trace the bottom and glue in place. Remove any air bubbles with a short section of the dowel. It is a good idea to dry fit the pieces first.

Before you place the lid on the box to dry, fold waxed paper to cover the entire top edge of the box, making sure it is wider than the depth of the lid. This step will prevent the two parts of the bandbox from sticking together. Allow to dry.

You can age your bandbox with a mixture of stain and varnish, with shoe polish, or with a paint wash. Do not overdo the aging. **Note:** When using wallpaper to cover a box, wheat wallpaper paste may work better than white glue.

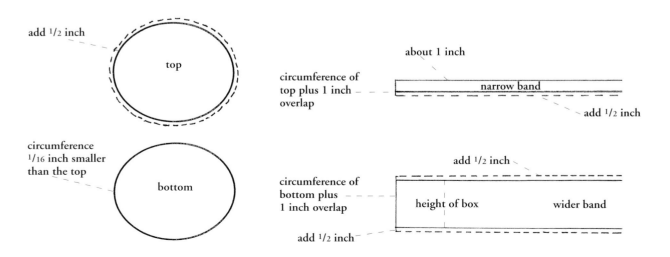

LAVENDER ORNAMENTS

Lavender-covered hearts, fans, and wreaths make unusual ornaments that you can use on a Christmas tree, as package ties, or in a window.

How to Make a Lavender Heart

Supplies and materials needed: 9-inch length of green thread-covered #18 gauge floral wire, 35mm film can, #26 gauge spool wire, waxed paper, 1/4-inch-wide ribbon, thick, tacky white glue, dried lavender blossoms, dried fairy roses and their buds or other small dried flowers, and foliage.

Bend the floral wire in half to form a right angle. Curve one end of the wire about halfway around the film can. Repeat with the other end of the wire. Cross the cut ends about 1/4 inch from the ends of the wire and secure them with a short piece of the spool wire. Lay the heart-shaped wire frame on the waxed paper.

Flatten or shape as necessary. Tie the ribbon around the top of the heart for a hanger.

Working with the heart on waxed paper, apply the glue to 2 to 3 inches of the heart at a time. Pour lavender blossoms onto the waxed paper and press the lavender into the glue, shaping the heart as you apply the blossoms. Continue to add more glue and blossoms until you cover the form. Finish shaping the heart and allow it to dry on the waxed paper. Attach a bow to the top and glue dried flowers on it.

Note: To make a wreath, form the floral wire into a circle using the film can. Secure the ends with spool wire and cover the circle with lavender. Glue a row of roses interspersed with sprigs of lavender on a bow and attach it. To make a fan, bend both ends of the floral wire 2 1/2 inches from each end to form two right angles. Bring the two cut ends together, overlap them by 1/4 inch, and secure them with spool wire. Cover the fan with lavender and bend the top into a bow. Glue ribbon pieces from the top to the base. Decorate with a bow with streamers, dried flowers, pieces of rosemary, and a rose placed in the center.

John Randolph, Virginia's last King's Attorney before the Revolution, noted in *A Treatise on Gardening* that lavender is "good in washing and bathing, as it scents the water and beautifies the flesh." These gift ideas suggest ways to use its scent in hangers or sachets to freshen closets and drawers.

How to Make a Lavender-Scented Padded Hanger

Supplies and materials needed: Wooden hanger, scissors, polyester sheet batting, white glue, dried lavender flowers, lavender oil, needle, white thread, and decorative fabric.

Measure the total length of the hanger. Cut two pieces of batting 36 inches long by half the length of the hanger plus 1/2 inch. Spread glue on half the width of the hanger, attach the edge of the first piece of batting, and wrap the batting around this width. Put lavender flowers and a drop of lavender oil on a strip of tissue. Roll the tissue lengthwise and tuck it between the layers of batting. Whip stitch the batting in place and close the end. Repeat on the other side.

Cut two strips of fabric 6 inches wide by the total length of the hanger. Fold the first strip lengthwise, turned wrong side out, and sew the long edge and one curved end together using a 1/4-inch seam. Turn the strip right side out and press. Repeat with the second strip. Slip the open end of the hanger into the opening in the fabric cover, gathering the fabric as you pull it over the batting. Repeat this process with the second fabric cover. Anchor the covers to the batting at each end of the hanger with small stitches and join the two sections in the middle on both sides of the hook with small stitches. Cut a piece of ribbon, double it over the center seam, and tie it into a bow to cover the seam.

How to Make a Lavender-Scented Padded Hanger with a Security Pocket

Supplies and materials needed: Wooden hanger, scissors, medium-weight polyester sheet batting, white glue, dried lavender flowers, lavender oil, needle, white thread, decorative fabric, and zipper.

To make a hanger with a pocket for jewelry and accessories, which is particularly handy for travelers, start by applying padding with lavender to a hanger as just described. Trace the curve of the top of the hanger on a piece of paper. Use this pattern to cut a piece of fabric the width of the tracing plus 3/4 inch on each side. Cut it 20 inches long. Cut across the width 5 inches from the curved section and install the zipper.

With the wrong side facing out and the two ends meeting at the curved top area, pin the two pieces together and sew up the sides using a 1/4-inch seam to the top center of the curved section. Leaving a small opening for the hook of the hanger, continue to sew down the other side to the fold line. Open the zipper and turn the fabric right side out and press. Put the hanger inside and bring the metal hook up through the opening in the top. Sew a line as close to the area below the hanger as possible by hand or by using the zipper foot on the sewing machine.

How to Make a Lavender Sachet

Supplies and materials needed: Decorative fabric, scissors, needle, thread, lavender oil, cotton ball, dried lavender flowers, and ribbon.

Cut a strip of fabric 10 x 8 inches. Fold the fabric lengthwise with the wrong side facing out. Sew around two open sides using a 1/4-inch seam. Turn and press the fabric, then turn the open end inside 5 inches. Put a drop of lavender oil on the cotton ball and insert it and dried lavender into the opening. Gather the sachet about 3 inches from the open end and tie it with a ribbon. Sew a small loop on the top of the sachet and put it over the hanger.

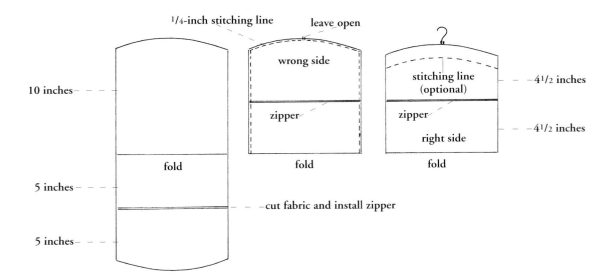

For the noncraftsperson who is anxious to give a special gift to a gardening friend, perhaps to mark a noteworthy occasion, here is an idea. This beautifully hand-painted document box is based on the design of a similar tin box in the collection of the Abby Aldrich Rockefeller Folk Art Museum. It is a handsome box to treasure by itself, but a visit to The Colonial Garden and Nursery yields packets of unusual seeds, linen twine, large wooden marking sticks, a bell jar (see page 3), and a rosemary topiary (see pages 32) in a clay pot. The box combined with any of these accessories and a few items from a garden center will delight the recipient.

How to Make a Hanging Lantern from a Williamsburg Bell Jar

This bell jar from The Colonial Garden and Nursery, the originals of which were used in the eighteenth century to protect tender seedlings, has been made into a hanging lantern to light a garden path.

Supplies and materials needed: Ty wire, heavy wire cutters, bell jar, pliers, chains, ring, votive candle in holder, and holder for hanging.

Cut a piece of wire the length of the area just under the lip of the jar plus 6 inches. Make a loop in one end of the wire using the pliers. Make four evenly spaced loops, based on the circumference under the lip, with the pliers. Ty wire is very strong. Wrap the wire under the lip of the jar and slip the straight end of the wire into the loop you formed at the other end. Bend the wire back from this loop with the pliers and twist to secure it. Bend the loops outward so the chain can hook into each of these four loops.

Measure the length of each chain you will need and open the links slightly so each is exactly the same length. Slip the open links into the loops and close the opening on the chain with pliers. Gather the loose ends of the chain and slip the open link ends onto the ring. Make sure the chain is not twisted and close the links in the chain.

Put a votive candle in the bottom of the lantern and hang on a crook-shaped holder. Use a long fireplace match to light the candle.

Conditioning and Arranging Plant Materials

If you carefully condition the greens and flowers you use, your efforts will be well rewarded, as they will remain fresh much longer. It does involve a little time and thought to gather plant materials with a good variety of color, textures, and sizes, but you will enjoy the results.

Always use clean containers. Household bleach will kill most bacteria and other organisms. Rinse the container well.

There are two basic types of floral preservatives: external floral shield products (antidesiccants) and general-purpose floral preservatives. External floral shield products, available through your florist or floral supply outlet, are designed to reduce moisture loss. They come in spray or powdered form. Follow the directions and either submerge the materials, such as a small wreath or branches, or spray your tree, wreath, plaque, or roping to extend the life of the greens.

General-purpose floral preservatives extend the vase life of flowers or foliage. Use them when conditioning and also when making an arrangement. These products contain a food sugar, an antibacterial agent to keep the water fresher for a longer period, and a wetting agent to aid in the uptake of water. It is also recommended to soak floral foam in a solution containing floral preservative. Use available floral dips; they are invaluable in conditioning some flowers such as Queen Anne's lace and bishop's weed. Other additives are listed under conditioning flowers.

It is a good idea to have on hand a supply of various gauges of floral and spool wire, floral pins, wired and unwired wooden picks, floral tapes, sharp clippers, wreath forms, clothesline wire, wire cutters, instant deluxe floral foam, and a variety of sizes of chicken feeders, plastic liners, floral foam cages, and other holders. With these supplies, you will be ready to tackle most projects.

At holiday time, cones, pods, and nuts will fare far better than fruit on an exterior wreath that faces the sun for much of the day. Balsam or spruce will not dry out and turn brown as quickly as white pine. If you live in an area where the temperatures are frequently below freezing, remember that most fruits are damaged and will change color when frozen. In Williamsburg, squirrels and birds also enjoy our fruit wreaths.

Before cutting or purchasing plant materials, be aware of protected species in your area. Do not use these materials even if they are available from a local vendor. This caution is especially true during the Christmas holidays.

CONDITIONING FOLIAGE

Evergreens with woody stems (holly, magnolia, pines, boxwood, firs, cedar): When you return from cutting, recut the stems at an angle and slit up from the cut end about 2 inches with sharp clippers or a knife. Submerge your materials, if possible, in warm water in a sink, large pail, or even a bathtub. The next day, cut the pieces to the desired length with the stems cut at an angle, remove all the foliage below the waterline, and stand the freshly cut stems upright in clean water. When dry, spray with an antidesiccant.

Evergreens with nonwoody stems (ivy, Alexandrian laurel, aucuba, cleyera): When you return from cutting, recut the stems at an angle, remove the foliage below the waterline, and stand the materials upright in water mixed with floral preservative overnight.

CONDITIONING FLOWERS

Cut flowers from your garden early in the morning or late in the afternoon. Carry a bucket of water with you for cut plant materials. Use very sharp, clean scissors or clippers. Whether bought or picked from your garden, as soon as you bring the flowers inside, remove all foliage below the water line and recut the stems at an angle. Immediately put them in clean containers of water with floral preservative. Allow them to rest overnight in a cool area. If possible, select flowers not yet fully opened. If using a refrigerator with automatic dehumidification (most modern ones), put the flowers in a tall, narrow vase and cover the blossoms very loosely with a plastic bag. Secure the bag around the base.

Use hot water to revive wilting flowers and warm water for those with soft stems. Mist frequently.

Woody-stemmed flowers from shrubs and flowering trees (azalea, lilac, dogwood, camellia): Cut the stems at an angle and split the stems with your clippers. Often dipping stems in boiling water for a few seconds will help. Azaleas, rhododendrons, and lilacs respond well to a dash of alcohol added to the warm conditioning water.

Lilies: Because stains from lily pollen are almost impossible to eliminate, remove the stamens before using blooming flowers. As buds open in the arrangement, remove the stamens.

Tulips: Recut the stems, insert a pin through the stem just below the flower, remove the lower leaves, and roll three or four stems at a time in newspaper to keep the stems straight. Stand upright in a deep, narrow container of warm water overnight or until used. Add a teaspoon of gin to the container.

Daffodils, hyacinths, and narcissi: Carry a container when picking and keep these flowers separate from others in shallow water for at least 2 hours. They exude a slimy sap that is damaging to other flowers. After conditioning, they can be added to an arrangement of mixed flowers. Cut off the white part at the base of any flowers that grow from bulbs. They do not like floral foam but do well in floral tubes or in small vases concealed in the arrangement.

Plants with milky, yellow, or colorless sap (poinsettia, euphorbia): Cut each stem and immediately singe it in a candle flame for 10 to 15 seconds. Poinsettias treated this way will last for 12 hours out of water, or they can be singed and put into water.

Roses: Remove the thorns and lower leaves and cut the stems underwater. Condition in hot water. To revive limp flowers, fill a sink with cool water and submerge them until they revive.

Ferns: Cut the fronds about 6 to 8 inches long and strip off the bottom 3 1/2 inches. Use a floral dip for 1 second and then place the ferns in a tall, narrow container. The container should be filled with water just below the foliage line.

TO COLOR SHEET MOSS GREEN

Spread yellowed or tan sheet moss on newspapers and dampen it on both sides with water from a spray bottle. Repeat several times until the sheet moss is thoroughly damp. Add some green food coloring to the water and spray it gradually on the top until it becomes green. Do this in stages so it does not become too green. If it does get too green, spray the moss with clear water to dilute the color. If the moss is very yellow, add a drop of blue to the green food coloring to help achieve a pleasant green color. **Note:** It is easier to work with the moss if it is damp.

GENERAL RULES OF ARRANGING

Cutting: Recut stems before using.

Conditioning: Condition all materials before arranging them according to the preceding instructions.

Size of materials: Keep the largest pieces near the center of the garland, plaque, or other arrangement and the lightest or smallest materials to the edges. Allow these light materials to extend out to give depth and distinction to your design.

Colors: Have colors well distributed throughout the arrangement, whether it is a cone, a wreath, roping, a Christmas tree, or a floral-filled epergne. Your colors must be balanced to be pleasing. Colors may be concentrated in the center or at the base of a flower arrangement. Use flowers to bring out the colors present in the room.

Flowers: Use all stages from bud stage to full bloom. Small buds extending out give depth; the full bloom stage is usually kept toward the center. Vary the texture of the materials.

Style: Try to reflect the style of the room—formal or informal.

Acknowledgments

This book is the third of its kind to be blessed with the photographic skills of Tom Green and the artistic talents of Betty Babb who did the color how-to illustrations. I am equally indebted to Helen M. Olds, senior book designer, for her consummate design skills, eye for color, and enthusiasm for this project. Special thanks are extended to Erin Michaela Bendiner, book editor/writer, for her diligent editorial assistance on the project, and Julie Watson, publications secretary, for her always cheerful and much appreciated assistance. Thanks also to Charles D. Anderson, John Ogden, and Cathy Swormstedt who proofread the designed pages.

Because it would not have been possible for one person to have designed and executed all the ideas presented here, it was my good fortune to be able to call on the talents and help of Clark Taggart, head of the Floral Design Studio for the Williamsburg Inn, and his staff: Wanda Ehly, Cora Garnett, Carey Savage, and volunteers Lis Doley and Nancy Parker. With Susan Winther's guidance in coordinating the fabrics and other details, they furnished floral arrangements for Tulipomania in Colonial Williamsburg's guesthouses for Historic Garden Week, the Draper's Dinner at the College of William and Mary, the dining room at the Coke-Garrett House, a New Year's Eve Dinner at the Lightfoot House, as well as Summer Weddings and A Winter Wedding Reception at the Williamsburg Inn. They also provided selected Christmas decorations.

It has been a wonderful experience to live for many years in or near the beautiful gardens of Colonial Williamsburg that are the inspiration for many of the ideas on these pages. I depended on Susan Dippre, supervisor for Historic Area landscape, Wesley Greene, garden historian, and Laura Viancour, coordinator, garden programs, for their knowledge of Colonial Williamsburg's gardens. In addition, Susan

and her landscape staff furnished plant materials whenever needed for special projects. Thanks to Susan and the help of gardeners James Bergmann, Robert Coles, Arthur Jones, Mark Jones, Kenny Mills, Wendy Saltzgiver, Charles Spruell, and Madelyn Young, the gardens were always ready when we photographed them. Wesley Greene and Don McKelvey, at The Colonial Garden and Nursery, give guests informative and fascinating interpretations of colonial gardening, highlights of which open this book. Laura Viancour's research into colonial fragrance gardens, potpourri, and sachets is included in the description of the fragrance garden and also in Gift Ideas. Gordon Chappell, director, landscape and facilities services, and staff members M. Kent Brinkley and Larry Griffith also gave advice and support.

I am grateful to the staff at the Williamsburg Inn for their cooperation during various endeavors at the Inn and in the guesthouses, including Clyde Min, general manager; Richard Tate and his Special Events staff; and Susan Winther and her staff in the Inn Design Studio. I am also grateful to Housekeeping who readied properties; Ann Carpenter and her staff in the Sewing Room; Ruth Hubbard who made the angels on the Angel Tree, and Hoy Correll, Robbie Hicks, Jason Marten, and Earl Warren for their help with the installation of Christmas trees for the Winter Wedding Reception, and Clark Taggart and the Floral Design Studio staff, mentioned earlier.

I would like to acknowledge other friends who provided arrangements including Betty Babb for the Floral-Decorated Hoop in Spring Ideas and the mantel and accompanying garland and the swag in Christmas Ideas; Valerie Hardy for the pumpkin snowman; Calvin Heikkila for the dried roses and hydrangea arrangement in Pyramids; Duryea Morton for his Dish Garden; Dianne Spence for the tiny pumpkin family and for help with the Hotch Potch Jumping Jack feather tree; and Barbara Stanley for the Bulbs in a Pot for Forcing. Information regarding plant preservation techniques was given to me by author and well-known arranger Georgia Vance who, with her assistant

Cathy Coyle, created the two dried-flower arrangements featured in Preserving Plant Materials. Special holiday touches include the pair of lady apple cones by the Craft House staff and the outdoor wreaths by Mary Hunter Curry, Iris Heissenbutl, Brenda Turner, and Carolyn Weekley in Christmas Ideas, and the decorations at the St. George Tucker House by Ann Bigoney and Joan Miller.

Special confectioneries and pastries by Judy Hornby, head pastry chef of the Colonial Williamsburg Company Hotel Group, assisted by Michelle Brown, pastry chef, and Roberta Lipford, pastry cook, are seen in Dessert in the Benjamin Waller House Gazebo, painted cookies on the Hotch Potch Christmas Tree, and at the Winter Wedding Reception. Rodney Diehl, pastry chef, also assisted with foods for the Winter Wedding Reception.

Thanks to the following who shared treasured recipes: Elizabeth Chambers for the Cookie Treetop Star; Harriet Hight for Nana's Raspberry Jam; Mildred Layne for Plantation Rum Punch; and the Williamsburg Inn for Granola and the Yule Log. From the Virginia Commonwealth Unit of the Herb Society of America, Cordelia P. Gabb, a founding member, contributed Hildegard's Nerve Cookies; and Elizabeth Crisp Rae, past president of the Herb Society of America, gave me the recipe for Fig-Sesame Jam. Kathy Chain and Bobbie Champaign kindly shared information on a variety of subjects including the late George Gross's mixture for Potpourri. Carmen Lancellotti gave advice about marzipan. Members of the unit's gourmet group were enthusiastic tasters for many of the recipes that appear here.

In Collections, Laura Pass Barry provided valuable information on prints, Margaret Beck Pritchard reviewed the text on decoupage, Janine Skerry identified containers and helped with nomenclature, Tanya Wilson advised on table settings. Don Thomas and Pat Waters facilitated photography in the museums. Phyllis Putnam at the Geddy site provided sources for information.

Thanks go to Colonial Williamsburg's photographers Dave Doody, Kelly Mihalcoe, and Lael White for additional photography; to Kathy Dunn, Cathy Grosfils, Mary Norment, and Tracey Stecklein for their scheduling assistance and locating transparencies; and to Mark Ragland for his photograph of a colorful bowl of peppers.

Special helpers deserve special thanks, including John Austin for assistance with setups and props; the Craft House staff for lending props; Lis Doley for assisting with the staging, food, and flowers for the Dessert in the Benjamin Waller House Gazebo and for the Winter Wedding Reception, and topiaries and cones for New Year's Eve Dinner at the Lightfoot House; Helen Dorsey for making arrangements for the use of properties; John Gonzales for his advice about pâtés and his help with last-minute food photography; and especially Dianne Spence for helping at many locations with props, food, and flowers, and as my right hand with the Angel Tree. All contributed in major ways to making this project more enjoyable and efficiently run.

Gift Ideas evolved from friends who helped. Bobbie Champaign graciously shared her lavender ornament instructions and Carol Harrison tested and furnished detailed directions for the Lavender-Scented Padded Hanger. A number of people helped test instructions for this section. Thanks to Betty Babb for painting the "Faux" Lead Finish on the terra-cotta pots; Rosemarie Rister McDonald and Sharyn Renaud Emerick who guided me through the making of a "Faux" Stone Trough; and Virginia P. Merrill for help with the decoupage watering can, plate, and vase.

Barbara Bilderback tested the instructions for the Christmas ornaments using quilt designs and Berit Mesarick provided patterns and reviewed my instructions for the Scandinavian Woven Hearts.

The following graciously permitted the use of their homes for photography: Mr. and Mrs. John Austin; President and Mrs. Colin Campbell, The Colonial Williamsburg Foundation; President and Mrs. Timothy Sullivan, the College of William and Mary; and Mr. and Mrs. Forrest Williamson. I feel fortunate to share scenes from these historic and interesting homes. Thanks also to Mr. and Mrs. Charles R. Longsworth for permission to photograph their daughter's summer wedding decorations.

Fellow miniaturists who contributed examples specifically for the miniature table settings in Spring are Nancy Clark, Pat and Bill Fifer, Jill Zimmerman. Lee-Ann Chellis Wessel made the finger vase and plates and Joep Suijker made and sent the fringed tulips from Holland.

A book of ideas benefits from special props. My thanks to Michelle Erickson, potter, for her special containers used in Tulipomania; Pat Fifer for her elegantly dressed angel holding an antique sensor that hangs above the mantel on the Christmas fireplace; Nancy Gotwald Harris for the basket of sachets; Carol Harrison for making several tablecloths; Diana Horton for her special embroidered tablecloths; Bettye Jean Lendrim for her beautifully painted document box in Gift Ideas; Jeff Rountree for his soup tureen and applesauce tart filled basket; Christopher Rountree for use of his special tree decked out for the birds; and Jill Zimmerman for her amusing Halloween hedgehog.

A special thanks goes to Richard McCluney for his continued support of this project, for which I am most grateful. Special thanks also go to Susan Winther who helped me in many ways to realize my far-flung ideas, and for her part in the wonderful projects on which we have worked. And finally to Joe, our sons Jeff and Christopher, and their families for their interest, encouragement, and good humor . . . in too many ways to recount.

Credits

page 100, Neapolitan-style angel, Enesco Corporation, Itasca, IL 60143.

page 109, Hildegard's Nerve Cookies recipe, reprinted from *Hildegard of Bingen's Medicine* by Dr. Wighard Strehlow & Gottfried Hetzka, M.D., published by Bear & Company, Inc., Rochester, VT 05767 Copyright © 1988 by Dr. Wighard Strehlow & Gottfried Hertzka, M.D.

page 112, Male and female northern Cardinals on Bittersweet branch in snowstorm © Gay Bumgarner/ Mira.com.

Index

Page numbers in **bold** refer to how-to instructions or recipes.